With the compliments
of the Artist
Hermann Fechenbach
1983

Yahweh said to Abram, 'Leave your country, your family and your father's house, for the land I will show you. I will make you a great nation; I will bless you and make your name so famous that it will be used as a blessing. I will bless those who bless you: I will curse those who slight you. All the tribes of the earth shall bless themselves by you.' *The First Book of Moses, 12. 1–3.*

MOSES

INTRODUCTION

The history of mankind gives evidence that every artist was inspired by the greatness of the Bible. I myself was already in my childhood fascinated by the stories of the Creation, Adam and Eve, the garden of Eden with the tree of knowledge of good and evil, Cain and Abel, Noah and the flood, the tower of Babel, Sodom and Gomorrah, Abraham, Isaac and Jacob, and as final ending of the first book of Moses, the grandiose story of Joseph and his brethren. So deep was my impression that I always had the longing to see illustrations of all those people. Simple as they were, deep inside they felt what was good or evil. Their close bond with God the Almighty was the sign that they were the chosen people. When I studied art and became acquainted with the technic of wood engraving, I realized with utter delight 'that is my medium'. Not only in because of its clear singular and impressive beauty of black and white, but also no other sort of illustration harmonizes so well with type, and it came to me like an invitation to create the stories of the first book of Moses, in wood engravings, although it took me many years to accomplish it.

H.F.

LET THERE BE LIGHT

⌒⌒⌒ CHAPTER 1. 1. In the beginning God created the heavens and the earth. 2. Now the earth was a formless void, there was darkness over the deep, and God's spirit hovered over the water. 3. God said, 'Let there be light', and there was light. 4. God saw that light was good, and God divided light from darkness. 5. God called light 'day', and darkness he called 'night'. Evening came and morning came: the first day.

THE DIVISION OF THE WATERS

6. God said, 'Let there be a vault in the waters to
divide the waters in two'. And so it was. 7. God made
the vault, and it divided the waters above the vault
from the waters under the vault. 8. God called the
vault 'heaven'. Evening came and morning came:
the second day.

THE DRY LAND

9. God said, 'Let the waters under heaven come together into a single mass, and let dry land appear'.
And so it was. 10. God called the dry land 'earth' and
the mass of waters 'seas', and God saw that it was
good. 11. God said, 'Let the earth produce vegetation:
seed-bearing plants, and fruit trees bearing fruit
with·their seed inside, on the earth'. And so it was.
12. The earth produced vegetation: plants bearing
seed in their several kinds, and trees bearing
fruit with their seed inside in their several kinds.
God saw that it was good. 13. Evening came and
morning came: the third day.

THE SUN AND THE MOON

14. God said, 'Let there be lights in the vault of heaven to divide day from night, and let them indicate festivals, days and years. 15. Let them be lights in the vault of heaven to shine on the earth'. And so it was. 16. God made the two great lights: the greater light to govern the day, the smaller light to govern the night, and the stars. 17. God set them in the vault of heaven to shine on the earth, 18. to govern the day and the night and to divide light from darkness. God saw that it was good. 19. Evening came and morning came: the fourth day.

FISH AND BIRDS

20. God said, 'Let the waters teem with living creatures, and let birds fly above the earth within the vault of heaven'. And so it was. 21. God created great sea-serpents and every kind of living creature with which the waters teem, and every kind of winged creature. God saw that it was good. 22. God blessed them, saying, 'Be fruitful, multiply, and fill the waters of the seas; and let the birds multiply upon the earth'. 23. Evening came and morning came: the fifth day.

THE CREATION OF MAN

24. God said, 'Let the earth produce every kind of living creature: cattle, reptiles, and every kind of wild beast'. And so it was. 25. God made every kind of wild beast, every kind of cattle, and every kind of land reptile. God saw that it was good. 26. God said, 'Let us make man in our own image, in the likeness of ourselves, and let them be masters of the fish of the sea, the birds of heaven, the cattle, all the wild beasts and all the reptiles that crawl upon the earth'. 27. God created man in the image of himself, in the image of God he created him, male and female he created them. 28. God blessed them, saying to them, 'Be fruitful, multiply, fill the earth and conquer it. Be masters of the fish of the sea, the birds of heaven and all living animals on the earth'. 29. God said, 'See, I give you all the seed-bearing plants that are upon the whole earth, and all the trees with seed-bearing fruit; this shall be your food. 30. To all wild beasts, all birds of heaven and all living reptiles on the earth I give all the foliage of plants for food.' And so it was. 31. God saw all he had

made, and indeed it was very good. Evening came and morning came: the sixth day.

THE SABBATH

⤳ CHAPTER 2. 1. Thus heaven and earth were completed with all their array. 2. On the seventh day God completed the work he had been doing. He rested on the seventh day after all the work he had been doing. 3. God blessed the seventh day and made it holy, because on that day he had rested after all his work of creating. 4. Such were the origins of heaven and earth when they were created. At the time when Yahweh God made earth and heaven 5. there was as yet no wild bush on the earth nor had any wild plant yet sprung up, for Yahweh God had not sent rain on the earth, nor was there any man to till the soil. 6. However, a flood was rising from the earth and watering all the surface of the soil. 7. Yahweh God fashioned man of dust from the soil. Then he breathed into his nostrils a breath of life, and thus man became a living being. 8. Yahweh God planted a garden in Eden which is in the east, and there he put the man he had fashioned. 9. Yahweh God caused to spring up from the soil every kind of tree, enticing to look at and good to eat, with the tree of life and the tree of the knowledge of good and evil in the middle of the garden. 10. A river flowed from Eden to water the garden, and from there it divided to make four streams. 11. The first is named the Pishon, and this encircles the whole land of Havilah where there is gold. 12. The gold of this land is pure; bdellium and onyx stone are found there. 13. The second river is named the Gihon, and this encircles the whole land of Cush. 14. The third river is named the Tigris, and this flows to the east of Ashur. The fourth river is the Euphrates. 15. Yahweh God took the man and settled him in the garden of Eden to cultivate and take care of it. 16. Then Yahweh God gave the man this admonition, 'You may eat indeed of all the trees in the garden. 17. Nevertheless of the tree of the knowledge of good and evil you are not to eat, for on the day you eat of it you shall most surely die'.

ADAM AND EVE

18. Yahweh God said, 'It is not good that the man should be alone. I will make him a helpmate'. 19. So from the soil Yahweh God fashioned all the wild beasts and all the birds of heaven. These he brought to the man to see what he would call them; each one was to bear the name the man would give it. 20. The man gave names to all the cattle, all the birds of heaven and all the wild beasts. But no helpmate suitable for man was found for him. 21. So Yahweh God made the man fall into a deep sleep. And while he slept, he took one of his ribs and enclosed it in flesh. 22. Yahweh God built the rib he had taken from the man into a woman, and brought her to the man. 23. The man exclaimed: 'This at last is bone from my bones, and flesh from my flesh! This is to be called woman, for this was taken from man.' 24. This is why a man leaves his father and mother and joins himself to his wife, and they become one body. 25. Now both of them were naked, the man and his wife, but they felt no shame in front of each other.

THE SERPENT

∽W∽ CHAPTER 3. 1. The serpent was the most subtle of all the wild beasts that Yahweh God had made. It asked the woman, 'Did God really say you were not to eat from any of the trees in the garden? 2. The woman answered the serpent, 'We may eat the fruit of the trees in the garden. 3. But of the fruit of the tree in the middle of the garden God said, "You must not eat it, nor touch it, under pain of death".' 4. Then the serpent said to the woman, 'No! You will not die! 5. God knows in fact that on the day you eat it your eyes will be opened and you will be like gods, knowing good and evil.' 6. The woman saw that the tree was good to eat and pleasing to the eye, and that it was desirable for the knowledge that it could give. So she took some of its fruit and ate it. She gave some also to her husband who was with her, and he ate it. 7. Then the eyes of both of them were opened and they realised that they were naked. So they sewed fig-leaves together to make themselves loin-cloths.

THE CURSE ON THE EARTH

8. The man and his wife heard the sound of Yahweh God walking in the garden in the cool of the day, and they hid from Yahweh God among the trees of the garden. 9. But Yahweh God called to the man. 'Where are you?' he asked. 10. 'I heard the sound of you in the garden;' he replied 'I was afraid because I was naked, so I hid.' 11. 'Who told you that you were naked?' he asked 'Have you been eating of the tree I forbade you to eat?' 12. The man replied, 'It was the woman you put with me; she gave me the fruit, and I ate it'. 13. Then Yahweh God asked the woman, 'What is this you have done?' The woman replied, 'The serpent tempted me and I ate'. 14. Then Yahweh God said to the serpent, 'Because you have done this, Be accursed beyond all cattle, all wild beasts. You shall crawl on your belly and eat dust every day of your life. 15. I will make you enemies of each other: you and the woman, your offspring and her offspring. It will crush your head and you will strike its heel.' 16. To the woman he said: 'I will multiply your pains in childbearing, you shall give

birth to your children in pain. Your yearning shall be for your husband, yet he will lord it over you.' 17. To the man he said, 'Because you listened to the voice of your wife and ate from the tree of which I had forbidden you to eat, 'Accursed be the soil because of you. With suffering shall you get your food from it every day of your life. 18. It shall yield you brambles and thistles, and you shall eat wild plants. 19. With sweat on your brow shall you eat your bread, until you return to the soil, as you were taken from it. For dust you are and to dust you shall return.' 20. The man named his wife 'Eve' because she was the mother of all those who live. 21. Yahweh God made clothes out of skins for the man and his wife, and they put them on.

Then Yahweh God said, 'See, the man has become like one of us, with his knowledge of good and evil.

BANISHMENT FROM EDEN

22. He must not be allowed to stretch his hand out next and pick from the tree of life also, and eat some and live for ever.' 23. So Yahweh God expelled him from the garden of Eden, to till the soil from which he had been taken. 24. He banished the man, and in front of the garden of Eden he posted the cherubs, and the flame of a flashing sword, to guard the way to the tree of life.

CAIN AND ABEL

꙰ CHAPTER 4. 1. The man had intercourse with his wife Eve, and she conceived and gave birth to Cain. 'I have acquired a man with the help of Yahweh' she said. 2. She gave birth to a second child, Abel, the brother of Cain. Now Abel became a shepherd and kept flocks, while Cain tilled the soil. 3. Time passed and Cain brought some of the produce of the soil as an offering for Yahweh, 4. while Abel for his part brought the first-born of his flock and some of their fat as well. Yahweh looked with favour on Abel and his offering. 5. But he did not look with favour on Cain and his offering, and Cain was very angry and downcast. 6. Yahweh asked Cain, 'Why are you angry and downcast? 7. If you are well disposed, ought you not to lift up your head? But if you are ill disposed, is not sin at the door like a crouching beast hungering for you, which you must master?'

THE FIRST MURDER

8. Cain said to his brother Abel, 'Let us go out'; and
while they were in the open country, Cain set on his
brother Abel and killed him. 9. Yahweh asked Cain,
'Where is your brother Abel?' 'I do not know' he
replied. 'Am I my brother's guardian?' 10. 'What
have you done?' Yahweh asked. 'Listen to the
sound of your brother's blood, crying out to me
from the ground.

THE CURSE ON CAIN

11. Now be accursed and driven from the ground that has opened its mouth to receive your brother's blood at your hands. 12. When you till the ground it shall no longer yield you any of its produce. You shall be a fugitive and a wanderer over the earth.' 13. Then Cain said to Yahweh, 'My punishment is greater than I can bear. 14. See! Today you drive me from this ground. I must hide from you, and be a fugitive and a wanderer over the earth. Why, whoever comes across me will kill me!' 15. 'Very well, then,' Yahweh replied 'if anyone kills Cain, sevenfold vengeance shall be taken for him.' So Yahweh put a mark on Cain, to prevent whoever might come across him from striking him down. 16. Cain left the presence of Yahweh and settled in the land of Nod, east of Eden.

ENOCH THE BUILDER

17. Cain had intercourse with his wife, and she conceived and gave birth to Enoch. He became builder of a town, and he gave the town the name of his son Enoch. 18. Enoch had a son, Irad, and Irad became the father of Mehujael; Mehujael became the father of Methushael, and Methushael became the father of Lamech. 19. Lamech married two women: the name of the first was Adah and the name of the second was Zillah.

JABAL THE SHEPHERD

20. Adah gave birth to Jabal: he was the ancestor of the tent-dwellers and owners of livestock.

JUBAL THE MUSICIAN

21. His brother's name was Jubal: he was the ancestor
of all who play the lyre and the flute.

TUBAL-CAIN THE METAL WORKER

22. As for Zillah, she gave birth to Tubal-cain: he was the ancestor of all metalworkers, in bronze or iron. Tubal-cain's sister was Naamah. 23. Lamech said to his wives: 'Adah and Zillah, hear my voice, Lamech's wives, listen to what I say: I killed a man for wounding me, a boy for striking me. 24. Sevenfold vengeance is taken for Cain, but seventy-sevenfold for Lamech.' 25. Adam had intercourse with his wife, and she gave birth to a son whom she named Seth, 'because God has granted me other offspring' she said 'in place of Abel, since Cain has killed him'. 26. A son was also born to Seth, and he named him Enosh. This man was the first to invoke the name of Yahweh.

CHAPTER 5. 1. This is the roll of Adam's descendants: On the day God created Adam he made him in the likeness of God. 2. Male and female he created them. He blessed them and gave them the name 'Man' on the day they were created. 3. When Adam was a hundred and thirty years old he became the father of a son, in his likeness, as his image, and he called him Seth. 4. Adam lived for eight hundred years after the birth of Seth and he became the father of sons and daughters. 5. In all, Adam lived for nine hundred and thirty years; then he died. 6. When Seth was a hundred and five years old he became the father of Enosh. 7. After the birth of Enosh, Seth lived for eight hundred and seven years, and he became the father of sons and daughters. 8. In all, Seth lived for nine hundred and twelve years; then he died. 9. When Enosh was ninety years old he became the father of Kenan. 10. After the birth of Kenan, Enosh lived for eight hundred and fifteen years and he became the father of sons and daughters. 11. In all, Enosh lived for nine hundred and five years; then he died. 12. When Kenan was seventy years old he became the father of Mahalalel. 13. After the birth of Mahalalel, Kenan lived for eight hundred and forty years and he became the father of sons and daughters. 14. In all, Kenan lived for nine hundred and ten years; then he died. 15. When Mahalalel was sixty-five years old he became the father of Jared. 16. After the birth of Jared, Mahalalel lived for eight hundred and thirty years and he became the father of sons and daughters. 17. In all, Mahalalel lived for eight hundred and ninety-five years; then he died. 18. When Jared was a hundred and sixty-two years old he became the father of Enoch. 19. After the birth of Enoch, Jared lived for eight hundred years and he became the father of sons and daughters. 20. In all, Jared lived for nine hundred and sixty-two years; then he died. 21. When Enoch was sixty-five years old he became the father of Methuselah. 22. Enoch walked with God. After the birth of Methuselah he lived for three hundred years and he became the father of sons and daughters. 23. In all, Enoch lived for three hundred and sixty-five years. 24. Enoch walked with God. Then he vanished because God took him. 25. When Methuselah was a hundred and eighty-seven years old he became the father of Lamech. 26. After the birth of Lamech, Methuselah lived for seven hundred and eighty-two years and he became the father of sons and daughters. 27. In all, Methuselah lived for nine hundred and sixty-nine years; then he died. 28. When Lamech was a hundred and eighty-two years old he became the father of a son. 29. He gave him the name Noah because, he said, 'Here is one who will give us, in the midst of our toil and the labouring of our hands, a consolation derived from the ground that Yahweh cursed.' 30. After the birth of Noah, Lamech lived for five hundred and ninety-five years and became the father of sons and daughters. 31. In all, Lamech lived for seven hundred and seventy-seven years; then he died. 32. When Noah was five hundred years old he became the father of Shem, Ham and Japheth.

THE STORY OF NOAH

CHAPTER 6. 1. When men had begun to be plentiful on the earth, and daughters had been born to them, 2. the sons of God, looking at the daughters of men, saw they were pleasing, so they married as many as they chose. 3. Yahweh said, 'My spirit must not for ever be disgraced in man, for he is but flesh; his life shall last no more than a hundred and twenty years'. 4. The Nephilim were on the earth at that time (and even afterwards) when the sons of God resorted to the daughters of man, and had children by them. These are the heroes of days gone by, the famous men. 5. Yahweh saw that the wickedness of man was great on the earth, and that the thoughts in his heart fashioned nothing but wickedness all day long. 6. Yahweh regretted having made man on the earth, and his heart grieved. 7. 'I will rid the earth's face of man, my own creation,' Yahweh said 'and of animals also, reptiles too, and the birds of heaven; for I regret having made them.' 8. But Noah had found favour with Yahweh. 9. This is the story of Noah: Noah was a good man, a man of integrity among his contemporaries, and he walked with God. 10. Noah became the father of three sons, Shem, Ham and Japheth. 11. The earth grew corrupt in God's sight, and filled with violence. 12. God contemplated the earth: it was corrupt, for corrupt were the ways of all flesh on the earth. 13. God said to Noah, 'The end has come for all things of flesh; I have decided this, because the earth is full of violence of man's making, and I will efface them from the earth. 14. Make yourself an ark out of resinous wood. Make it with reeds and line it with pitch inside and out. 15. This is how to make it: the length of the ark is to be three hundred cubits, its breadth fifty cubits, and its height thirty cubits. 16. Make a roof for the ark… put the door of the ark high up in the side, and make a first, second and third deck. 17. 'For my part I mean to bring a flood, and send the waters over the earth, to destroy all flesh on it, every living creature under heaven; everything on earth shall perish. 18. But I will establish my Covenant with you, and you must go on board the ark, yourself, your sons, your wife, and your sons' wives along with you. 19. From all living creatures, from all flesh, you must take two of each kind aboard the ark, to save their lives with yours; they must be a male and a female. 20. Of every kind of bird, of every kind of animal and of every kind of reptile on the ground, two must go with you so that their lives may be saved. 21. For your part provide yourself with eatables of all kinds, and lay in a store of them, to serve as food for yourself and them.' 22. Noah did this; he did all that God had ordered him.

TWO OF EACH KIND

◦w◦ CHAPTER 7. 1. Yahweh said to Noah, 'Go aboard the ark, you and all your household, for you alone among this generation do I see as a good man in my judgement. 2. Of all the clean animals you must take seven of each kind, both male and female; of the unclean animals you must take two, a male and its female 3. (and of the birds of heaven also, seven of each kind, both male and female), to propagate their kind over the whole earth. 4. For in seven days' time I mean to make it rain on the earth for forty days and nights, and I will rid the earth of every living thing that I made.' 5. Noah did all that Yahweh ordered. 6. Noah was six hundred years old when the flood of waters appeared on the earth. 7. Noah with his sons, his wife, and his sons' wives boarded the ark to escape the waters of the flood. 8. (Of the clean animals and the animals that are not clean, of the birds and all that crawls on the ground, 9. two of each kind boarded the ark with Noah, a male and a female, according to the order God gave Noah.) 10. Seven days later the waters of the flood appeared on the earth. 11. In the six hundredth year of Noah's life, in the second month, and on the seventeenth day of that month, that very day all the springs of the great deep broke through, and the sluices of heaven opened. 12. It rained on the earth for forty days and forty nights. 13. That very day Noah and his sons Shem, Ham and Japheth boarded the ark, with Noah's wife and the three wives of his sons, 14. and with them wild beasts of every kind, cattle of every kind, reptiles of every kind that crawls on the earth, birds of every kind, all that flies, everything with wings. 15. One pair of all that is flesh and has the breath of life boarded the ark with Noah; 16. and so there went in a male and a female of every creature that is flesh, just as God had ordered him. And Yahweh closed the door behind Noah.

THE FLOOD

17. The flood lasted forty days on the earth. The waters swelled, lifting the ark until it was raised above the earth. 18. The waters rose and swelled greatly on the earth, and the ark sailed on the waters. 19. The waters rose more and more on the earth so that all the highest mountains under the whole of heaven were submerged. 20. The waters rose fifteen cubits higher, submerging the mountains. 21. And so all things of flesh perished that moved on the earth, birds, cattle, wild beasts, everything that swarms on the earth, and every man. 22. Everything with the breath of life in its nostrils died, everything on dry land. 23. Yahweh destroyed every living thing on the face of the earth, man and animals, reptiles, and the birds of heaven. He rid the earth of them, so that only Noah was left, and those with him in the ark. 24. The waters rose on the earth for a hundred and fifty days.

THE OLIVE BRANCH

CHAPTER 8. 1. But God had Noah in mind, and all the wild beasts and all the cattle that were with him in the ark. God sent a wind across the earth and the waters subsided. 2. The springs of the deep and the sluices of heaven were stopped. Rain ceased to fall from heaven; 3. the waters gradually ebbed from the earth. After a hundred and fifty days the waters fell, 4. and in the seventh month, on the seventeenth day of that month, the ark came to rest on the mountains of Ararat. 5. The waters gradually fell until the tenth month when, on the first day of the tenth month, the mountain peaks appeared. 6. At the end of forty days Noah opened the porthole he had made in the ark 7. and he sent out the raven. This went off, and flew back and forth until the waters dried up from the earth. 8. Then he sent out the dove, to see whether the waters were receding from the surface of the earth. 9. The dove, finding nowhere to perch, returned to him in the ark, for there was water over the whole surface of the earth; putting out his hand he took hold of it and brought it back into the ark with him. 10. After waiting seven more days, again he sent out the dove from the ark. 11. In the evening, the dove came back to him and there it was with a new olive-branch in its beak. So Noah realised that the waters were receding from the earth. 12. After waiting seven more days he sent out the dove, and now it returned to him no more. 13. It was in the six hundred and first year of Noah's life, in the first month and on the first of the month, that the water dried up from the earth. Noah lifted back the hatch of the ark and looked out. The surface of the ground was dry! 14. In the second month and on the twenty-seventh day of the month the earth was dry.

GOD'S COVENANT

15. Then God said to Noah, 16. 'Come out of the ark, you yourself, your wife, your sons, and your son's wives with you. 17. As for all the animals with you, all things of flesh, whether birds or animals or reptiles that crawl on the earth, bring them out with you. Let them swarm on the earth; let them be fruitful and multiply on the earth.' 18. So Noah went out with his sons, his wife, and his sons' wives. 19. And all the wild beasts, all the cattle, all the birds and all the reptiles that crawl on the earth went out from the ark, one kind after another. 20. Noah built an altar for Yahweh, and choosing from all the clean animals and all the clean birds he offered burnt offerings on the altar. 21. Yahweh smelt the appeasing fragrance and said to himself, 'Never again will I curse the earth because of man, because his heart contrives evil from his infancy. Never again will I strike down every living thing as I have done. 22. As long as earth lasts, sowing and reaping, cold and heat, summer and winter, day and night shall cease no more.'

CHAPTER 9. 1. God blessed Noah and his sons, saying to them, 'Be fruitful, multiply and fill the earth. 2. Be the terror and the dread of all the wild beasts and all the birds of heaven, of everything that crawls on the ground and all the fish of the sea; they are handed over to you. 3. Every living and crawling thing shall provide food for you, no less than the foliage of plants. I give you everything, 4. with this exception: you must not eat flesh with life, that is to say blood, in it. 5. I will demand an account of your life-blood. I will demand an account from every beast and from man. I will demand an account of every man's life from his fellow men. 6. He who sheds man's blood, shall have his blood shed by man, for in the image of God man was made. 7. As for you, be fruitful, multiply, teem over the earth and be lord of it.' 8. God spoke to Noah and his sons, 9. 'See, I establish my Covenant with you, and with your descendants after you; 10. also with every living creature to be found with you, birds, cattle and every wild beast with you: everything that came out of the ark, everything that lives on the earth. 11. I establish my Covenant with you: no thing of flesh shall be swept away again by the waters of the flood. There shall be no flood to destroy the earth again.' 12. God said, 'Here is the sign of the Covenant I make between myself and you and every living creature with you for all generations: 13. I set my bow in the clouds and it shall be a sign of the Covenant between me and the earth. 14. When I gather the clouds over the earth and the bow appears in the clouds, 15. I will recall the Covenant between myself and you and every living creature of every kind. And so the waters shall never again become a flood to destroy all things of flesh. 16. When the bow is in the clouds I shall see it and call to mind the lasting Covenant between God and every living creature of every kind that is found on the earth.' 17. God said to Noah, 'This is the sign of the Covenant I have established between myself and every living thing that is found on the earth'.

HAM'S MISFORTUNE

18. The sons of Noah who went out from the ark were Shem, Ham and Japheth; Ham is the ancestor of the Canaanites. 19. These three were Noah's sons, and from these the whole earth was peopled. 20. Noah, a tiller of the soil, was the first to plant the vine. 21. He drank some of the wine, and while he was drunk he uncovered himself inside his tent. 22. Ham, Canaan's ancestor, saw his father's nakedness, and told his two brothers outside.

THE CURSE ON CANAAN

23. Shem and Japheth took a cloak and they both put it over their shoulders, and walking backwards, covered their father's nakedness; they kept their faces turned away, and did not see their father's nakedness. 24. When Noah awoke from his stupor he learned what his youngest son had done to him. 25. And he said: 'Accursed be Canaan. He shall be his brothers' meanest slave.' 26. He added: 'Blessed be Yahweh, God of Shem, let Canaan be his slave! 27. May God extend Japheth, may he live in the tents of Shem, and may Canaan be his slave!' 28. After the flood Noah lived three hundred and fifty years. 29. In all, Noah's life lasted nine hundred and fifty years; then he died.

CHAPTER 10. 1. These are the descendants of Noah's sons, Shem, Ham and Japheth, to whom sons were born after the flood: 2. Japheth's sons: Gomer, Magog, the Medes, Javan, Tubal, Meshech, Tiras. 3. Gomer's sons: Ashkenaz, Riphath, Togarmah. 4. Javan's sons: Elishah, Tarshish, the Kittim, the Dananites. 5. From these came the dispersal to the islands of the nations. These were Japheth's sons, according to their countries and each of their languages, according to their tribes and their nations. 6. Ham's sons: Cush, Misraim, Put, Canaan. 7. Cush's sons: Seba, Havilah, Sabtah, Raamah, Sabteca. Raamah's sons: Sheba, Dedan. 8. Cush became the father of Nimrod who was the first potentate on earth. 9. He was a mighty hunter in the eyes of Yahweh, hence the saying, 'Like Nimrod, a mighty hunter in the eyes of Yahweh'. 10. First to be included in his empire were Babel, Erech and Accad, all of them in the land of Shinar. 11. From this country came Ashur, the builder of Nineveh, Rehoboth-ir, Calah, 12. and Resen between Nineveh and Calah (this is the great city). 13. Misraim became the father of the people of Lud, of Anam, Lehab, Naphtuh, 14. Pathros, Casluh and Caphtor, from which the Philistines came. 15. Canaan became the father of Sidon, his first-born, then Heth, 16. and the Jebusites, the Amorites, Girgashites, 17. Hivites, Arkites, Sinites, 18. Arvadites, Zemarites, Hamathites; later the Canaanite tribes scattered. 19. The Canaanite frontier stretched from Sidon in the direction of Gerar and as far as Gaza, then in the direction of Sodom, Gomorrah, Admah and Zeboim, and as far as Lesha. 20. These were Ham's sons, according to their tribes and languages, according to their countries and nations. 21. Shem also was the father of children, the ancestor of all the sons of Eber and the elder brother of Japheth. 22. Shem's sons: Elam, Asshur, Arpachshad, Lud, Aram. 23. Aram's sons: Uz, Hul, Gether and Mash. 24. Arpachshad became the father of Shelah, and Shelah became the father of Eber. 25. To Eber were born two sons: the first was called Peleg, because it was in his time that the earth was divided, and his brother was called Joktan. 26. Joktan became the father of Almodad, Sheleph, Hazarmaveth, Jerah, 27. Hadoram, Uzal, Diklah, 28. Obal, Abima-el, Sheba, 29. Ophir, Havilah, Jobab; all these are sons of Joktan. 30. They occupied a stretch of country from Mesha in the direction of Sephar, the eastern mountain range. 31. These were Shem's sons, according to their tribes and languages, and according to their countries and nations. 32. These were the tribes of Noah's sons, according to their descendants and their nations. From these came the dispersal of the nations over the earth, after the flood.

THE TOWER OF BABEL

◦〰◦ CHAPTER 11. 1. Throughout the earth men spoke the same language, with the same vocabulary. 2. Now as they moved eastwards they found a plain in the land of Shinar where they settled. 3. They said to one another, 'Come, let us make bricks and bake them in the fire'. — For stone they used bricks, and for mortar they used bitumen. — 4. 'Come,' they said 'let us build ourselves a town and a tower with its top reaching heaven. Let us make a name for ourselves, so that we may not be scattered about the whole earth.' 5. Now Yahweh came down to see the town and the tower that the sons of man had built. 6. 'So they are all a single people with a single language!' said Yahweh. 'This is but the start of their undertakings! There will be nothing too hard for them to do. 7. Come, let us go down and confuse their language on the spot so that they can no longer understand one another.' 8. Yahweh scattered them thence over the whole face of the earth, and they stopped building the town. 9. It was named Babel therefore, because there Yahweh confused the language of the whole earth. It was from there that Yahweh scattered them over the whole face of the earth. 10. These are Shem's descendants: When Shem was a hundred years old he became the father of Arpachshad, two years after the flood. 11. After the birth of Arpachshad, Shem lived five hundred years and became the father of sons and daughters. 12. When Arpachshad was thirty-five years old he became the father of Shelah. 13. After the birth of Shelah, Arpachshad lived four hundred and three years and became the father of sons and daughters. 14. When Shelah was thirty years old he became the father of Eber. 15. After the birth of Eber, Shelah lived four hundred and three years and became the father of sons and daughters. 16. When Eber was thirty-four years old he became the father of Peleg. 17. After the birth of Peleg, Eber lived four hundred and thirty years and became the father of sons and daughters. 18. When Peleg was thirty years old he became the father of Reu. 19. After the birth of Reu, Peleg lived two hundred and nine years and became the father of sons and daughters. 20. When Reu was thirty-two years old he became the father of Serug. 21. After the birth of Serug, Reu lived two hundred and seven years and became the father of sons and daughters. 22. When Serug was thirty years old he became the father of Nahor. 23. After the birth of Nahor, Serug lived two hundred years and became the father of sons and daughters. 24. When Nahor was twenty-nine years old he became the father of Terah. 25. After the birth of Terah, Nahor lived a hundred and nineteen years and became the father of sons and daughters. 26. When Terah was seventy years old he became the father of Abram, Nahor and Haran. 27. These are Terah's descendants: Terah became the father of Abram, Nahor and Haran. Haran became the father of Lot. 28. Haran died in the presence of his father Terah in his native land, Ur of the Chaldaeans. 29. Abram and Nahor both married: Abram's wife was called Sarai, Nahor's wife was called Milcah, the daughter of Haran, father of Milcah and Iscah. 30. Sarai was barren, having no child. 31. Terah took his son Abram, his grandson Lot the son of Haran, and his daughter-in-law the wife of Abram, and made them leave Ur of the

Chaldaeans to go to the land of Canaan. But on arrival in Haran they settled there. 32. Terah's life lasted two hundred and five years; then he died at Haran.

ABRAM AND LOT

CHAPTER 12. 1. Yahweh said to Abram, 'Leave your country, your family and your father's house, for the land I will show you. 2. I will make you a great nation; I will bless you and make your name so famous that it will be used as a blessing. 3. I will bless those who bless you: I will curse those who slight you. All the tribes of the earth shall bless themselves by you.' 4. So Abram went as Yahweh told him, and Lot went with him. Abram was seventy-five years old when he left Haran. 5. Abram took his wife Sarai, his nephew Lot, all the possessions they had amassed and the people they had acquired in Haran. They set off for the land of Canaan, and arrived there. 6. Abram passed through the land as far as Shechem's holy place, the Oak of Moreh. At that time the Canaanites were in the land. 7. Yahweh appeared to Abram and said, 'It is to your descendants that I will give this land'. So Abram built there an altar for Yahweh who had appeared to him. 8. From there he moved on to the mountainous district east of Bethel, where he pitched his tent, with Bethel to the west and Ai to the east. There he built an altar to Yahweh and invoked the name of Yahweh. 9. Then Abram made his way stage by stage to the Negeb. 10. When famine came to the land Abram went down into Egypt to stay there for the time, since the land was hard pressed by the famine. 11. On the threshold of Egypt he said to his wife Sarai, 'Listen! I know you are a beautiful woman. 12. When the Egyptians see you they will say, "That is his wife", and they will kill me but spare you. 13. Tell them you are my sister, so that they may treat me well because of you and spare my life out of regard for you.' 14. When Abram arrived in Egypt the Egyptians did indeed see that the woman was very beautiful. 15. When Pharaoh's officials saw her they sang her praises to Pharaoh and the woman was taken into Pharaoh's palace. 16. He treated Abram well because of her, and he received flocks, oxen, donkeys, men and women slaves, she-donkeys and camels. 17. But Yahweh inflicted severe plagues on Pharaoh and his household because of Abram's wife Sarai. 18. So Pharaoh summoned Abram and said, 'What is this you have done to me? Why did you not tell me she was your wife? 19. Why did you say, "She is my sister", so that I took her for my wife? Now, here is your wife. Take her and go! 20. Pharaoh committed him to men who escorted him back to the frontier with his wife and all he possessed.

LOT'S CHOICE

CHAPTER 13. 1. From Egypt Abram returned to the Negeb with his wife and all he possessed, and Lot with him. 2. Abram was a very rich man, with lifestock, silver and gold. 3. By stages he went from the Negeb to Bethel, where he had first pitched his tent, between Bethel and Ai, 4. at the place where he had formerly erected the altar. Here Abram invoked the name of Yahweh. 5. Lot, who was travelling with Abram, had flocks and cattle of his own, and tents too. 6. The land was not sufficient to accommodate them both at once, for they had too many possessions to be able to live together. 7. Dispute broke out between the herdsmen of Abram's livestock and those of Lot's. (The Canaanites and the Perizzites were then living in the land.) 8. Accordingly Abram said to Lot, 'Let there be no dispute between me and you, nor between my herdsmen and yours, for we are brothers. 9. Is not the whole land open before you? Part company with me: if you take the left, I will go right; if you take the right, I will go left.' 10. Looking round, Lot saw all the Jordan plain, irrigated everywhere—this was before Yahweh destroyed Sodom and Gomorrah—like the garden of Yahweh or the land of Egypt, as far as Zoar. 11. So Lot chose all the Jordan plain for himself and moved off eastwards. Thus they parted company: 12. Abram settled in the land of Canaan; Lot settled among the towns of the plain, pitching his tents on the outskirts of Sodom. 13. Now the people of Sodom were vicious men, great sinners against Yahweh. 14. Yahweh said to Abram after Lot had parted company with him, 'Look all round from where you are towards the north and the south, towards the east and the west. 15. All the land within sight I will give to you and your descendants for ever. 16. I will make your descendants like the dust on the ground: when men succeed in counting the specks of dust on the ground, then they will be able to count your descendants! 17. Come, travel through the length and breadth of the land, for I mean to give it to you.' 18. So Abram went with his tents to settle at the Oak of Mamre, at Hebron, and there he built an altar to Yahweh.

ABRAM LEARNS OF LOT'S DEFEAT

〰〰 CHAPTER 14. 1. It was in the time of Amraphel king of Shinar, Arioch king of Ellasar, Chedor-
laomer king of Elam, and Tidal king of the Goiim.
2. These made war on Bera king of Sodom, Birsha
king of Gomorrah, Shinab king of Admah, Shemeber
king of Zeboiim, and the king of Bela (that is, Zoar).
3. These latter all banded together in the Valley of
Siddim (that is, the Salt Sea). 4. For twelve years
they had been under the yoke of Chedor-laomer, but
in the thirteenth year they revolted. 5. In the four-
teenth year Chedor-laomer arrived and the kings who
were on his side. They defeated the Rephaim at
Asteroth-karnaim, the Zuzim at Ham, the Emim in
the plain of Kiriathaim, 6. the Horites in the mountainous district of Seir as far as El-paran, which is on
the edge of the wilderness. 7. Wheeling round, they
came to the Spring of Judgement (that is, Kadesh);
they conquered all the territory of the Amalekites
and also the Amorites who lived in Hazazon-tamar.
8. Then the kings of Sodom, Gomorrah, Admah,
Zeboiim and Bela (that is, Zoar) marched out and

took up battle positions against them in the Valley of Siddim, 9. against Chedor-laomer king of Elam, Tidal king of the Goiim, Amraphel king of Shinar and Arioch king of Ellasar: four kings against five! 10. Now there were many bitumen wells in the Valley of Siddim, and in their flight the kings of Sodom and Gomorrah fell into them, while the rest took refuge in the mountains. 11. The conquerors seized all the possessions of Sodom and Gomorrah, and all their provisions, and made off. 12. They also took Lot (the nephew of Abram) and his possessions and made off; he was living at Sodom. 13. A survivor came to tell Abram the Hebrew, who was living at the Oak of the Amorite Mamre, the brother of Eshcol and Aner; these were allies of Abram.

MELCHIZEDEK WELCOMES ABRAM

14. When Abram heard that his kinsman had been taken captive, he mustered his supporters, the members of his household from birth, numbering three hundred and eighteen, and led them in pursuit as far as Dan. 15. He and his servants fell on them by night and defeated them, pursuing them as far as Hobah, north of Damascus. 16. He recaptured all the goods, along with his kinsman Lot and his possessions, together with the women and people. 17. When Abram came back after the defeat of Chedor-laomer and the kings who had been on his side, the king of Sodom came to meet him in the Valley of Shaveh (that is, the Valley of the King). 18. Melchizedek king of Salem brought bread and wine; he was a priest of God Most High. 19. He pronounced this blessing: 'Blessed be Abram by God Most High, creator of heaven and earth, 20. and blessed be God Most High for handing over your enemies to you'. And Abram gave him a tithe of everything.

THE KING OF SODOM

21. The king of Sodom said to Abram, 'Give me the people and take the possessions for yourself'. 22. But Abram replied to the king of Sodom, 'I raise my hand in the presence of Yahweh, God Most High, creator of heaven and earth: 23. not one thread, not one sandal strap, nothing will I take of what is yours; you shall not say, "I enriched Abram". 24. For my-self, nothing. There is only what my men have eaten, and the share belonging to the men who came with me, Eshkol, Aner and Mamre; let them take their share.'

ABRAM'S VISION

〜w〜 CHAPTER 15. 1. It happened some time later that the word of Yahweh was spoken to Abram in a vision, 'Have no fear, Abram, I am your shield; your reward will be very great'. 2. My Lord Yahweh', Abram replied 'what do you intend to give me? I go childless...' 3. Then Abram said, 'See, you have given me no descendants; some man of my household will be my heir'. 4. And then this word of Yahweh was spoken to him, 'He shall not be your heir; your heir shall be of your own flesh and blood'. 5. Then taking him outside he said, 'Look up to heaven and count the stars if you can. Such will be your descendants' he told him. 6. Abram put his faith in Yahweh, who counted this as making him justified. 7. 'I am Yahweh' he said to him 'who brought you out of Ur of the Chaldaeans to make you heir to this land.' 8. 'My Lord Yahweh,' Abram replied 'how am I to know that I shall inherit it?'

YAHWEH'S PROMISE

9. He said to him, 'Get me a three-year-old heifer, a three-year-old goat, a three-year-old ram, a turtle-dove and a young pigeon'. 10. He brought him all these, cut them in half and put half on one side and half facing it on the other; but the birds he did not cut in half. 11. Birds of prey came down on the carcases but Abram drove them off. 12. Now as the sun was setting Abram fell into a deep sleep, and terror seized him. 13. Then Yahweh said to Abram, 'Know this for certain, that your descendants will be exiles in a land not their own, where they will be slaves and oppressed for four hundred years. 14. But I will pass judgement also on the nation that enslaves them and after that they will leave, with many possessions. 15. For your part, you shall go to your fathers in peace; you shall be buried at a ripe old age. 16. In the fourth generation they will come back here, for the wickedness of the Amorites is not yet ended.' 17. When the sun had set and darkness had fallen, there appeared a smoking furnace and a firebrand that went between the halves. 18. That day Yahweh

made a Covenant with Abram in these terms: 'To your descendants I give this land, from the wadi of Egypt to the Great River, the river Euphrates, 19. the Kenites, the Kenizzites, the Kadmonites, 20. the Hittites, the Perizzites, the Rephaim, 21. the Amorites, the Canaanites, the Girgashites, and the Jebusites.'

SARAI AND THE SLAVE GIRL

CHAPTER 16. 1. Abram's wife Sarai had borne him no child, but she had an Egyptian maid-servant named Hagar. 2. So Sarai said to Abram, 'Listen, now! Since Yahweh has kept me from having children, go to my slave-girl. Perhaps I shall get children through her.' Abram agreed to what Sarai had said. 3. Thus after Abram had lived in the land of Canaan for ten years Sarai took Hagar her Egyptian slave-girl and gave her to Abram as his wife.

HAGAR

4. He went to Hagar and she conceived. And once she
knew she had conceived, her mistress counted for
nothing in her eyes. 5. Then Sarai said to Abram
'May this insult to me come home to you! It was I
who put my slave-girl into your arms but now she
knows that she has conceived, I count for nothing in
her eyes. Let Yahweh judge between me and you.'
6. 'Very well,' Abram said to Sarai 'your slave-girl is
at your disposal. Treat her as you think fit.' Sarai
accordingly treated her so badly that she ran away
from her.

HAGAR AND THE ANGEL

7. The angel of Yahweh met her near a spring in the wilderness, the spring that is on the road to Shur. 8. He said, 'Hagar, slave-girl of Sarai, where have you come from, and where are you going?' 'I am running away from my mistress Sarai' she replied. 9. The angel of Yahweh said to her, 'Go back to your mistress and submit to her'. 10. The angel of Yahweh said to her, 'I will make your descendants too numerous to be counted'. 11. Then the angel of Yahweh said to her: 'Now you have conceived, and you will bear a son, and you shall name him Ishmael, for Yahweh has heard your cries of distress. 12. A wild-ass of a man he will be, against every man, and every man against him, setting himself to defy all his brothers.' 13. Hagar gave a name to Yahweh who had spoken to her: 'You are El Roi', for, she said, 'Surely this is a place where I, in my turn, have seen the one who sees me?' 14. This is why this well is called the well of Lahai Roi; it is between Kadesh and Bered. 15. Hagar bore Abram a son, and Abram gave to

the son that Hagar bore the name Ishmael. 16. Abram
was eighty-six years old when Hagar bore him Ishmael.

༺ఌ CHAPTER 17. 1. When Abram was ninety-nine
years old Yahweh appeared to him and said, 'I am El
Shaddai. Bear yourself blameless in my presence,
2. and I will make a Covenant between myself and
you, and increase your numbers greatly.' 3. Abram
bowed to the ground and God said this to him, 4.
'Here now is my covenant with you: you shall become
the father of a multitude of nations. 5. You shall no
longer be called Abram; your name shall be Abraham,
for I make you father of a multitude of nations. 6. I
will make you most fruitful. I will make you into
nations, and your issue shall be kings. 7. I will
establish my Covenant between myself and you, and
your descendants after you, generation after generation, a Covenant in perpetuity, to be your God and the
God of your descendants after you. 8. I will give to you
and to your descendants after you the land you are
living in, the whole land of Canaan, to own in perpetuity, and I will be your God.' 9. God said to
Abraham, 'You on your part shall maintain my
Covenant, yourself and your descendants after you,
generation after generation. 10. Now this is my
Covenant which you are to maintain between myself
and you, and your descendants after you: all your
males must be circumcised. 11. You shall circumcise
your foreskin, and this shall be the sign of the Covenant between myself and you. 12. When they are
eight days old all your male children must be circumcised, generation after generation of them, no matter
whether they be born within the household or bought
from a foreigner not one of your descendants. 13.
They must always be circumcised, both those born
within the household and those who have been bought.
My Covenant shall be marked on your bodies as a
Covenant in perpetuity. 14. The uncircumcised male,
whose foreskin has not been circumcised, such a man
shall be cut off from his people: he has violated my
Covenant.' 15. God said to Abraham, 'As for Sarai
your wife, you shall not call her Sarai, but Sarah.
16. I will bless her and moreover give you a son by
her. I will bless her and nations shall come out of her;
kings of peoples shall descend from her.' 17. Abraham

bowed to the ground, and he laughed, thinking to himself, 'Is a child to be born to a man one hundred years old, and will Sarah have a child at the age of ninety?' 18. Abraham said to God, 'Oh, let Ishmael live in your presence!' 19. But God replied, 'No, but your wife Sarah shall bear you a son whom you are to name Isaac. With him I will establish my Covenant, a Covenant in perpetuity, to be his God and the God of his descendants after him. 20. For Ishmael too I grant you your request: I bless him and I will make him fruitful and greatly increased in numbers. He shall be the father of twelve princes, and I will make him into a great nation. 21. But my Covenant I will establish with Isaac, whom Sarah will bear you at this time next year.' 22. When he had finished speaking to Abraham God went up from him. 23. Then Abraham took his son Ishmael, all those born in his household and all those he had bought, in short all the males among the people of Abraham's household, and circumcised their foreskins that same day, in accordance with God's commands to him. 24. Abraham was ninety-nine years old when his foreskin was circumcised. 25. Ishmael his son was thirteen years old when his foreskin was circumcised. 26. That same day Abraham and his son Ishmael were circumcised; 27. all the men of his household, both those born in the household and those who had been bought, were circumcised with him.

THREE MEN AT MAMRE

CHAPTER 18. 1. Yahweh appeared to him at the Oak of Mamre while he was sitting by the entrance of the tent during the hottest part of the day. 2. He looked up, and there he saw three men standing near him. As soon as he saw them he ran from the entrance of the tent to meet them, and bowed to the ground. 3. 'My lord,' he said 'I beg you, if I find favour with you, kindly do not pass your servant by. 4. A little water shall be brought; you shall wash your feet and lie down under the tree. 5. Let me fetch a little bread and you shall refresh yourselves before going further. That is why you have come in your servant's direction.' They replied, 'Do as you say'. 6. Abraham hastened to the tent to find Sarah. 'Hurry,' he said 'knead three bushels of flour· and make loaves.' 7. Then running to the cattle Abraham took a fine and tender calf and gave it to the servant, who hurried to prepare it. 8. Then taking cream, milk and the calf he had prepared, he laid all before them, and they ate while he remained standing near them under the tree.

THE PROMISE OF ISAAC

9. 'Where is your wife Sarah?' they asked him. 'She is in the tent' he replied. 10. Then his guest said, 'I shall visit you again next year without fail, and your wife will then have a son'. Sarah was listening at the entrance of the tent behind him. 11. Now Abraham and Sarah were old, well on in years, and Sarah had ceased to have her monthly periods. 12. So Sarah laughed to herself, thinking, 'Now that I am past the age of child-bearing, and my husband is an old man, is pleasure to come my way again!' 13. But Yahweh asked Abraham, 'Why did Sarah laugh and say, "Am I really going to have a child now that I am old?" 14. Is anything too wonderful for Yahweh? At the same time next year I shall visit you again and Sarah will have a son.' 15. 'I did not laugh' Sarah said, lying because she was afraid. But he replied, 'Oh yes, you did laugh'. 16. From there the men set out and arrived within sight of Sodom, with Abraham accompanying them to show them the way. 17. Now Yahweh had wondered, 'Shall I conceal from Abraham what I am going to do, 18. seeing that Abraham will

become a great nation with all the nations of the
earth blessing themselves by him? 19. For I have
singled him out to command his sons and his household after him to maintain the way of Yahweh by
just and upright living. In this way Yahweh will carry
out for Abraham what he has promised him.'

ABRAHAM PLEADS FOR SODOM

20. Then Yahweh said, 'How great an outcry there is against Sodom and Gomorrah! How grievous is their sin! 21. I propose to go down and see whether or not they have done all that is alleged in the outcry against them that has come up to me. I am determined to know.' 22. The men left there and went to Sodom while Abraham remained standing before Yahweh. 23. Approaching him he said, 'Are you really going to destroy the just man with the sinner? 24. Perhaps there are fifty just men in the town. Will you really overwhelm them, will you not spare the place for the fifty just men in it? 25. Do not think of doing such a thing: to kill the just man with the sinner, treating just and sinner alike! Do not think of it! Will the judge of the whole earth not administer justice?' 26. Yahweh replied, 'If at Sodom I find fifty just men in the town, I will spare the whole place because of them'. 27. Abraham replied, 'I am bold indeed to speak like this to my Lord, I who am dust and ashes. 28. But perhaps the fifty just men lack five: will you destroy the whole city for five?' 'No,'

he replied 'I will not destroy it if I find forty-five just men there.' 29. Again Abraham said to him, 'Perhaps there will only be forty there'. 'I will not do it' he replied 'for the sake of the forty.' 30. Abraham said, 'I trust my Lord will not be angry, but give me leave to speak: perhaps there will only be thirty there'. 'I will not do it' he replied 'if I find thirty there.' 31. He said, 'I am bold indeed to speak like this, but perhaps there will only be twenty there'. 'I will not destroy it' he replied 'for the sake of the twenty.' 32. He said, 'I trust my Lord will not be angry if I speak once more: perhaps there will only be ten'. 'I will not destroy it' he replied 'for the sake of the ten.' 33. When he had finished talking to Abraham Yahweh went away, and Abraham returned home.

THE SODOMITES

CHAPTER 19. 1. When the two angels reached Sodom in the evening, Lot was sitting at the gate. As soon as Lot saw them he rose to meet them and bowed to the ground. 2. 'I beg you, my lords,' he said 'please come down to your servant's house to stay the night and wash your feet. Then in the morning you can continue your journey.' 'No,' they replied 'we can spend the night in the open street.' 3. But he pressed them so much that they went home with him and entered his house. He prepared a meal for them, baking unleavened bread, and they ate. 4. They had not gone to bed when the house was surrounded by the men of the town, the men of Sodom both young and old, all the people without exception. 5. Calling to Lot they said, 'Where are the men who came to you tonight? Send them out to us so that we may abuse them.' 6. Lot came out to them at the door, and having closed the door behind him said, 7. 'I beg you, my brothers, do no such wicked thing. 8. Listen, I have two daughters who are virgins. I am ready to send them out to you, to treat as it pleases you. But as for the men, do nothing to them, for they have come under the shadow of my roof.' 9. But they replied, 'Out of the way! Here is one who came as a foreigner, and would set himself up as a judge. Now we will treat you worse than them.' Then they forced Lot back and moved forward to break down the door. 10. But the men reached out, pulled Lot back into the house, and shut the door. 11. And they struck the men who were at the door of the house with blindness, from youngest to oldest, and they never found the doorway.

THE DESTRUCTION OF SODOM

12. The men said to Lot, 'Have you anyone else here?
Your sons, your daughters and all your people in the
town, take them out of the place. 13. We are about
to destroy this place, for there is a great outcry
against them, and it has reached Yahweh. And Yahweh has sent us to destroy them.' 14. Lot went to
speak to his future sons-in-law who were to marry
his daughters. 'Come,' he said 'leave this place, for
Yahweh is about to destroy the town.' But his sons-
in-law thought he was joking. 15. When dawn broke
the angels urged Lot, 'Come, take your wife and these
two daughters of yours, or you will be overwhelmed
in the punishment of the town'. 16. And as he hesi-
tated, the men took him by the hand, and his
wife and his two daughters, because of the pity
Yahweh felt for him. They led him out and left
him outside the town.

LOT'S ESCAPE

17. As they were leading him out he said, 'Run for
your life. Neither look behind you nor stop anywhere
on the plain. Make for the hills if you would not be
overwhelmed.' 18. 'No, I beg you, my lord,' Lot said
to them 19. 'your servant has won your favour and
you have shown great kindness to me in saving my
life. But I could not reach the hills before this cala-
mity overtook me, and death with it. 20. The town
over there is near enough to flee to, and is a little one.
Let me make for that—is it not little?—and my life
will be saved.' 21. He answered, 'I grant you this
favour too, and will not destroy the town you speak
of. 22. Hurry, escape to it, for I can do nothing until
you reach it.' That is why the town is named Zoar.

LOT'S WIFE

23. As the sun rose over the land and Lot entered Zoar, 24. Yahweh rained on Sodom and Gomorrah brimstone and fire from Yahweh. 25. He overthrew these towns and the whole plain, with all the inhabitants of the towns, and everything that grew there. 26. But the wife of Lot looked back, and was turned into a pillar of salt. 27. Rising early in the morning Abraham went to the place where he had stood before Yahweh, 28. and looking towards Sodom and Gomorrah, and across all the plain, he saw the smoke rising from the land, like smoke from a furnace. 29. Thus it was that when God destroyed the towns of the plain, he kept Abraham in mind and rescued Lot out of disaster when he overwhelmed the towns where Lot lived. 30. After leaving Zoar Lot settled in the hill country with his two daughters, for he dared not stay at Zoar. He made his home in a cave, himself and his two daughters.

LOT'S DESCENDANTS

31. The elder said to the younger, 'Our father is an old man, and there is not a man in the land to marry us in the way they do the world over. 32. Come let us ply our father with wine and sleep with him. In this way we shall have children by our father.' 33. That night they made their father drunk, and the elder slept with her father though he was unaware of her coming to bed or of her leaving. 34. The next day the elder said to the younger, 'Last night I slept with my father. Let us make him drunk again tonight, and you go and sleep with him. In this way we shall have children by our father. 35. They made their father drunk that night too, and the younger went and slept with him, but he was unaware of her coming to bed or of her leaving. 36. Both Lot's daughters thus became pregnant by their father. 37. The elder gave birth to a son whom she named Moab; and he is the ancestor of the Moabites of our own times. 38. The younger also gave birth to a son whom she named Ben-ammi; and he is the ancestor of the Bene-ammon of our own times.

74

CHAPTER **20**. 1. Abraham left there for the land of the Negeb, and settled between Kadesh and Shur, staying for the time being at Gerar. 2. Of his wife Sarah, Abraham said, 'She is my sister', and Abimelech the king of Gerar had Sarah brought to him, 3. But God visited Abimelech in a dream at night. 'You are to die' he told him 'because of the woman you have taken, for she is a married woman.' 4. Abimelech however had not gone near her; so he said, 'My Lord, would you kill innocent people too?' 5. Did he not tell me himself, "She is my sister", and did not she herself say, "He is my brother"?' I did this with a clear conscience and clean hands.' 6. 'Yes I know' God replied in the dream 'that you did this with a clear conscience, and it was I who prevented you from sinning against me. That was why I did not let you touch her. 7. Now send the man's wife back; for he is a prophet and can intercede on your behalf for your life. But understand that if you do not send her back, you will most surely die, and all your people too.' 8. So Abimelech rose early next morning and summoning all his servants told them the whole story, at which the men were very much afraid. 9. Then summoning Abraham Abimelech said to him, 'What have you done to us? What wrong have I done you that you bring so great a sin on me and on my kingdom? You have treated me as you should not have done.' 10. And Abimelech asked Abraham, 'What possessed you to do this?' 11. 'Because' Abraham replied 'I thought there would be no fear of God here; and the people would kill me because of my wife. 12. Besides, she is indeed my sister, my father's daughter though not my mother's; and she became my wife. 13. So when God made me wander far from my father's home I said to her, "There is a kindness you can do me: everywhere we go, say of me that I am your brother".' 14. Abimelech took sheep, cattle, men and women slaves, and presented them to Abraham, and gave him back his wife Sarah. 15. And Abimelech said, 'See, my land lies before you. Settle wherever you please.' 16. To Sarah he said, 'Look, I am giving one thousand pieces of silver to your brother. For you this will be compensation in the eyes of all those with you...' 17. At Abraham's prayer God healed Abimelech, his wife and his slave-girls,

so that they could have children, 18. for Yahweh had
made all the women of Abimelech's household barren
on account of Sarah, Abraham's wife.

ISAAC AND ISHMAEL

⟨꙳⟩ CHAPTER **21**. 1. Yahweh dealt kindly with Sarah as he had said, and did what he had promised her. 2. So Sarah conceived and bore a son to Abraham in his old age, at the time God had promised. 3. Abraham named the son born to him Isaac, the son to whom Sarah had given birth. 4. Abraham circumcised his son Isaac when he was eight days old, as God had commanded him. 5. Abraham was a hundred years old when his son Isaac was born to him. 6. Then Sarah said, 'God has given me cause to laugh; all those who hear of it will laugh with me'. 7. She added: 'Who would have told Abraham that Sarah would nurse children! Yet I have borne him a child in his old age.' 8. The child grew and was weaned. and Abraham gave a great banquet on the day Isaac was weaned. 9. Now Sarah watched the son that Hagar the Egyptian had borne to Abraham, playing with her son Isaac. 10. 'Drive away that slave-girl and her son,' she said to Abraham; 'this slave-girl's son is not to share the inheritance with my son Isaac.'

THE DEPARTURE OF HAGAR

11. This greatly distressed Abraham because of his son, 12. but God said to him, 'Do not distress yourself on account of the boy and your slave-girl. Grant Sarah all she asks of you, for it is through Isaac that your name will be carried on. 13. But the slave-girl's son I will also make into a nation, for he is your child too.' 14. Rising early next morning Abraham took some bread and a skin of water and, giving them to Hagar, he put the child on her shoulder and sent her away. She wandered off into the wilderness of Beer-sheba.

HAGAR'S DISTRESS

15. When the skin of water was finished she abandoned the child under a bush. 16. Then she went and sat down at a distance, about a bowshot away, saying to herself, 'I cannot see the child die'. So she sat at a distance; and the child wailed and wept.

GOD'S PROMISE TO HAGAR

17. But God heard the boy wailing, and the angel of God called to Hagar from heaven. 'What is wrong, Hagar?' he asked. 'Do not be afraid, for God has heard the boy's cry where he lies. 18. Come, pick up the boy and hold him safe, for I will make him into a great nation.' 19. Then God opened Hagar's eyes and she saw a well, so she went and filled the skin with water and gave the boy a drink. 20. God was with the boy. He grew up and made his home in the wilderness, and he became a bowman. 21. He made his home in the wilderness of Paran, and his mother chose him a wife from the land of Egypt.

ABRAHAM AND ABIMELECH

22. At that time Abimelech came with Phicol, the commander of his army, to speak to Abraham, 'God is with you in all you are doing. 23. Swear by God to me here and now that you will not trick me, neither myself nor my descendants nor any of mine, and that you will show the same kindness to me and the land of which you are a guest as I have shown to you.' 24. 'Yes,' Abraham replied 'I swear it.' 25. Abraham reproached Abimelech about a well that Abimelech's servants had seized. 26. 'I do not know who has done this' Abimelech said. 'You yourself have never mentioned it to me and, for myself, I heard nothing of it till today.' 27. Then Abraham took sheep and cattle and presented them to Abimelech and the two of them made a covenant. 28. Abraham put seven lambs of the flock on one side. 29. 'Why have you put these seven lambs on one side?' Abimelech asked Abraham. 30. He replied, 'You must accept these seven lambs from me as evidence that I have dug this well.' 31. This is why they called that place Beersheba, because there the two of them swore an oath. 32.

After they had made a covenant at Beersheba Abimelech went off with Phicol, the commander of his
army, and returned to the land of the Philistines.
33. Abraham planted a tamarisk at Beersheba and
there he invoked Yahweh, the everlasting God.
34. Abraham stayed for a long while in the land
of the Philistines.

GOD TESTS ABRAHAM

᠍᠍᠍᠍᠍᠍᠍᠍᠍᠍᠍᠍ CHAPTER **22**. 1. It happened some time later that God put Abraham to the test. 'Abraham, Abraham' he called. 'Here I am' he replied. 2. 'Take your son,' God said 'your only child Isaac, whom you love, and go to the land of Moriah. There you shall offer him as a burnt offering, on a mountain I will point out to you.' 3. Rising early next morning Abraham saddled his ass and took with him two of his servants and his son Isaac. He chopped wood for the burnt offering and started on his journey to the place God had pointed out to him. 4. On the third day Abraham looked up and saw the place in the distance. 5. Then Abraham said to his servants, 'Stay here with the donkey. The boy and I will go over there; we will worship and come back to you.'

ABRAHAM AND ISAAC

6. Abraham took the wood for the burnt offering,
loaded it on Isaac, and carried in his own hands the
fire and the knife. Then the two of them set out together. 7. Isaac spoke to his father Abraham, 'Father'
he said. 'Yes, my son' he replied. 'Look,' he said 'here
are the fire and the wood, but where is the lamb for
the burnt offering?' 8. Abraham answered, 'My son,
God himself will provide the lamb for the burnt
offering'. Then the two of them went on together.
9. When they arrived at the place God had pointed
out to him, Abraham built an altar there, and
arranged the wood. Then he bound his son Isaac and
put him on the altar on top of the wood.

YAHWEH RENEWS HIS PROMISE

10. Abraham stretched out his hand and seized the knife to kill his son. 11. But the angel of Yahweh called to him from heaven. 'Abraham, Abraham' he said. 'I am here' he replied. 12. 'Do not raise your hand against the boy' the angel said. 'Do not harm him, for now I know you fear God. You have not refused me your son, your only son.' 13. Then looking up, Abraham saw a ram caught by its horns in a bush. Abraham took the ram and offered it as a burnt-offering in place of his son. 14. Abraham called this place 'Yahweh provides', and hence the saying today: On the mountain Yahweh provides. 15. The angel of Yahweh called Abraham a second time from heaven. 16. 'I swear by my own self—it is Yahweh who speaks —because you have done this, because you have not refused me your son, your only son, 17. I will shower blessings on you, I will make your descendants as many as the stars of heaven and the grains of sand on the seashore. Your descendants shall gain possession of the gates of their enemies. 18. All the nations of the earth shall bless themselves by your descen-

dants, as a reward for your obedience.' 19. Abraham
went back to his servants, and together they set out
for Beersheba, and he settled in Beersheba. 20. It
happened some time later that Abraham received
word that Milcah, too, had now borne sons to his
brother Nahor: 21. Uz his first-born, Buz his brother,
Kemuel Aram's father, 22. Chesed, Hazo, Pildash,
Jidlaph, Bethuel 23. (and Bethuel was the father of
Rebekah). These are the eight children Milcah gave
Nahor, Abraham's brother. 24. He had a concubine
named Reumah, and she too had children: Tebah,
Gaham, Tahash and Maacah.

THE DEATH OF SARAH

⌒⌒⌒ CHAPTER 23. 1. The length of Sarah's life was a hundred and twenty-seven years. 2. She died at Kiriath-arba, or Hebron, in the land of Canaan, and Abraham went in to mourn and grieve for her. 3. Then leaving his dead, Abraham spoke to the sons of Heth: 4. 'I am a stranger and a settler among you' he said. 'Let me own a burial-plot among you, so that I may take my dead wife and bury her.'

ABRAHAM PURCHASES A BURIAL GROUND

5. The sons of Heth gave Abraham this answer, 6. 'Listen, my lord, you are God's prince amongst us; bury your dead in the best of our tombs; not one of us would refuse you his tomb and keep you from burying your dead'. 7. Abraham rose and bowed to the ground before the people of the land, the sons of Heth, 8. and spoke to them. 'If' he said 'you are willing for me to take my dead wife and bury her, then listen to me. Intercede for me with Ephron, Zohar's son, 9. to give me the cave he owns at Machpelah, which is on the edge of his land. Let him make it over to me in your presence at its full price, for me to own as a burial-plot.' 10. Now Ephron was sitting among the sons of Heth, and Ephron the Hittite answered Abraham in the hearing of the sons of Heth and of all the citizens of the town. 11. 'My lord, listen to me' he said. 'I give you the land and I give you the cave on it; I make this gift in the sight of the sons of my people. Bury your dead.' 12. Abraham bowed before the people of the land 13. and he spoke to Ephron in the hearing of the

people of the land, 'Oh, if it be you... But listen to me. I will pay the price of the land; accept it from me and I will bury my dead there.' 14. Ephron answered Abraham, 15. 'My lord, listen to me. A property worth four hundred shekels of silver, what is a little thing like that between me and you? Bury your dead.' 16. Abraham agreed to Ephron's terms, and Abraham weighed out for Ephron the silver he had stipulated in the hearing of the sons of Heth, namely four hundred shekels of silver, according to the current commercial rate. 17. Thus Ephron's field at Machpelah opposite Mamre, the field and the cave that was on it, and all the trees that were on it, the whole of its extent in every direction, passed 18. into Abraham's possession in the sight of the sons of Heth and of all the citizens of the town. 19. After this Abraham buried his wife Sarah in the cave of the field of Machpelah opposite Mamre, in the country of Canaan. 20. And so the field and the cave that was on it passed from the sons of Heth into Abraham's possession to be owned as a burial-plot.

ABRAHAM DESIRES A WIFE FOR ISAAC

CHAPTER 24. 1. By now Abraham was an old man well on in years, and Yahweh had blessed him in every way. 2. Abraham said to the eldest servant of his household, the steward of all his property, 'Place your hand under my thigh, 3. I would have you swear by Yahweh, God of heaven and God of earth, that you will not choose a wife for my son from the daughters of the Canaanites among whom I live. 4. Instead, go to my own land and my own kinsfolk to choose a wife for my son Isaac.' 5. The servant asked him, 'What if the woman does not want to come with me to this country? Must I take your son back to the country from which you came?' 6. Abraham answered, 'On no account take my son back there. 7. Yahweh, God of heaven and God of earth, took me from my father's home, and from the land of my kinsfolk, and he swore to me that he would give this country to my descendants. He will now send his angel ahead of you, so that you may choose a wife for my son there. 8. And if the woman does not want to come with you, you will be free from this oath of mine. Only do not take my son back there.' 9. And the servant placed his hand under the thigh of his master Abraham, and swore to him that he would do it.

ABRAHAM'S SERVANT'S PRAYER

10. The servant took ten of his master's camels and
something of the best of all his master owned, and
set out for Aram Naharaiim and the town of Nahor.
11. In the evening, at the time when women go down
to draw water, he made the camels kneel outside the
town near the well. 12. And he said, 'Yahweh, God of
my master Abraham, be with me today, and show
your kindness to my master Abraham. 13. Here I
stand by the spring as the young women from the
town come out to draw water. 14. To one of the girls
I will say: Please tilt your pitcher and let me drink.
If she answers, "Drink, and I will water your camels
too", may she be the one you have chosen for your
servant Isaac; by this I shall know you have shown
your kindness to my master.'

REBEKAH

15. He had not finished speaking when Rebekah came
out. She was the daughter of Bethuel, son of Milcah,
wife of Abraham's brother Nahor. She had a pitcher
on her shoulder. 16. The girl was very beautiful, and
a virgin; no man had touched her. She went down to
the spring, filled her pitcher and came up again.
17. Running to meet her, the servant said, 'Please give
me a little water to drink from your pitcher'. 18.
She replied, 'Drink, my lord', and she quickly lowered her pitcher on her arm and gave him a drink.
19. When she had finished letting him drink, she
said, 'I will draw water for your camels, too, until
they have had enough'.

REBEKAH WATERS THE CAMELS

20. She quickly emptied her pitcher into the trough,
and ran to the well again to draw water, and drew
water for all the camels 21. while the man watched
in silence, wondering whether Yahweh had made his
journey successful or not. 22. When the camels had
finished drinking, the man took a gold ring weighing
half a shekel, and put it through her nostrils, and put
on her arms two bracelets weighing ten gold shekels,
23. and he said, 'Whose daughter are you? Please tell
me. Is there room at your father's house for us to
spend the night?' 24. She answered, 'I am the daughter of Bethuel, the son whom Milcah bore to Nahor'.
25. And she went on, 'We have plenty of straw and
fodder, and room to lodge'. 26. Then the man bowed
down and worshipped Yahweh 27. saying, 'Blessed be
Yahweh, God of my master Abraham, for he has not
stopped showing kindness and goodness to my master. Yahweh has guided my steps to the house of my
master's brother.' 28. The girl ran to her mother's
house to tell what had happened. 29. Now Rebekah
had a brother called Laban, and Laban ran out to

the man at the spring. 30. As soon as he had seen the ring and the bracelets his sister was wearing, and had heard his sister Rebekah saying, 'This is what the man said to me', he went to the man and found him still standing by his camels at the spring.

LABAN'S INVITATION

31. He said to him, 'Come in, blessed of Yahweh, why stay out here when I have cleared the house and made room for the camels?' 32. The man went to the house, and Laban unloaded the camels. He provided straw and fodder for the camels and water for him and his companions to wash their feet. 33. They offered him food, but he said, 'I will eat nothing before I have said what I have to say'. Laban said, 'Speak'. 34. He said, 'I am the servant of Abraham. 35. Yahweh has overwhelmed my master with blessings, and Abraham is now very rich. He has given him flocks and herds, silver and gold, men slaves and women slaves, camels and donkeys. 36. Sarah, my master's wife, bore him a son in his old age, and he has made over all his property to him. 37. My master made me take this oath, "You are not to choose a wife for my son from the daughters of the Canaanites in whose country I live. 38. Curse you if you do not go to my father's home and to my kinsfolk to choose a wife for my son." 39. I said to my master: Suppose the woman will not agree to come with me? 40. and his reply was, "Yah-

weh, in whose presence I have walked, will send his
angel to make your journey successful; you shall
choose a wife for my son from my kinsfolk and from
my father's house. 41. So doing, you will be free from
my curse: you will have gone to my family, and if
they refuse you, you will be free from my curse.'
42. Arriving today at the spring I said: Yahweh, God
of my master Abraham, show me, I pray, if you intend to make my journey successful. 43. Here I stand,
by the spring: when a girl comes out to draw water
and I say to her: Please let me drink a little water
from your pitcher, 44. and she replies, "Drink by all
means, and I will draw water for your camels too",
may she be the wife Yahweh has chosen for my
master's son: 45. I was still turning this over in my
mind when Rebekah came out, her pitcher on her
shoulder. She came down to the spring and drew
water. I said to her: Please give me a drink. 46.
Quickly she lowered her pitcher saying, "Drink, and
I will water your camels too". 47. I asked her: Whose
daughter are you? She replied, "I am the daughter
of Bethuel, whom Milcah bore to Nahor". Then I put
this ring through her nostrils and these bracelets on
her arms. 48. I bowed down and worshipped Yahweh,
and I blessed Yahweh, God of my master Abraham,
who had so graciously led me to choose the daughter
of my master's brother for his son. 49. Now tell me
whether you are prepared to show kindness and goodness to my master; if not, say so, and I shall know
what to do.' 50. Laban and Bethuel replied, 'This is
from Yahweh; it is not in our power to say yes or no
to you. 51. Rebekah is there before you. Take her and
go; and let her become the wife of your master's son,
as Yahweh has decreed.' 52. On hearing this Abraham's servant prostrated himself on the ground
before Yahweh. 53. He brought out silver and gold
ornaments and clothes which he gave to Rebekah; he
also gave rich presents to her brother and to her
mother. 54. They ate and drank, he and his companions, and they spent the night there. Next morning when they were up, he said, 'Let me go back to
my master'.

REBEKAH'S DEPARTURE

55. Rebekah's brother and mother replied, 'Let the girl stay with us a few days, perhaps ten; after that she may go'. 56. But he replied, 'Do not delay me; it is Yahweh who has made my journey successful; let me leave to go back to my master'. 57. They replied, 'Let us call the girl and find out what she has to say'. 58. They called Rebekah and asked her, 'Do you want to leave with this man?' 'I do' she replied. 59. Accordingly they let their sister Rebekah go, with her nurse, and Abraham's servant and his men. 60. They blessed Rebekah in these words: 'Sister of ours, increase to thousands and tens of thousands! May your descendants gain possession of the gates of their enemies!' 61. Rebekah and her servants stood up, mounted the camels, and followed the man. The servant took Rebekah and departed.

REBEKAH MEETS ISAAC

62. Isaac, who lived in the Negeb, had meanwhile come into the wilderness of the well of Lahai Roi. 63. Now Isaac went walking in the fields as evening fell, and looking up saw camels approaching. 64. And Rebekah looked up and saw Isaac. She jumped down from her camel, 65. and asked the servant, 'Who is that man walking through the fields to meet us?' The servant replied, 'That is my master'; then she took her veil and hid her face.

REBEKAH BECOMES ISAAC'S WIFE

66. The servant told Isaac the whole story, 67. and Isaac led Rebekah into his tent and made her his wife; and he loved her. And so Isaac was consoled for the loss of his mother.

ABRAHAM AND KETURAH

⟨∿⟩ CHAPTER 25. 1. Abraham married another wife whose name was Keturah; 2. and she bore him Zimram, Jokshan, Medan, Midian, Ishbak and Shuah. —3. Jokshan was the father of Sheba and Dedan, and the sons of Dedan were the Asshurites, the Letushim and the Leummim.—4. The sons of Midian are Ephah, Epher, Hanoch, Abida and Eldaah. All these are sons of Keturah.

THE DEATH OF ABRAHAM

5. Abraham gave all his possessions to Isaac. 6. To the sons of his concubines Abraham gave presents, and during his lifetime he sent them away from his son Isaac eastward, to the east country. 7. The number of years Abraham lived was a hundred and seventy-five. 8. Then Abraham breathed his last, dying at a ripe old age, an old man who had lived his full span of years; and he was gathered to his people.

ABRAHAM'S BURIAL

9. His sons Isaac and Ishmael buried him in the cave of Machpelah opposite Mamre, in the field of Ephron the Hittite, son of Zohar. 10. This was the field that Abraham had bought from the sons of Heth, and Abraham and his wife Sarah were buried there. 11. After Abraham's death God blessed his son Isaac, and Isaac lived near the well of Lahai Roi. 12. These are the descendants of Ishmael, the son of Abraham by Hagar, Sarah's Egyptian maidservant. 13. These are the names of the sons of Ishmael in the order of their birth: Ishmael's first born was Nebaioth; then Kedar, Adbeel, Mibsam, 14. Mishma, Dumah, Massa, 15. Hadad, Tema, Jetur, Naphish and Kedemah. 16. These are the sons of Ishmael, and these are their names, according to their settlements and encampments, twelve chiefs of as many tribes. 17. The number of years Ishmael lived was one hundred and thirty-seven. Then he breathed his last, died, and was gathered to his people. 18. He lived in the territory

stretching from Havilah to Shur, which is to the east
of Egypt, on the way to Assyria. He set himself to
defy his brothers.

ISAAC'S PRAYER

19. This is the story of Isaac son of Abraham. Abraham was the father of Isaac. 20. Isaac was forty years old when he married Rebekah, the daughter of Bethuel the Aramaean of Paddan-aram, and sister of Laban the Aramaean. 21. Isaac prayed to Yahweh on behalf of his wife, for she was barren. Yahweh heard his prayer, and his wife Rebekah conceived. 22. But the children struggled with one another inside her, and she said, 'If this is the way of it, why go on living?' So she went to consult Yahweh, 23. and he said to her: 'There are two nations in your womb, your issue will be two rival peoples. One nation shall have the master of the other, and the elder shall serve the younger.'

THE BIRTH OF ESAU AND JACOB

24. When the time came for her confinement, there
were indeed twins in her womb. 25. The first to be
born was red, and as though he were completely
wrapped in a hairy cloak; so they named him Esau.
26. Then his brother was born, with his hand grasping
Esau's heel; so they named him Jacob. Isaac was
sixty years old at the time of their birth.

ESAU

27. When the boys grew up Esau became a skilled hunter, a man of the open country.

JACOB

Jacob on the other hand was a quiet man, staying at home among the tents. 28. Isaac preferred Esau, for he had a taste for wild game; but Rebekah preferred Jacob.

ESAU YIELDS HIS BIRTHRIGHT

29. Once, Jacob had made a soup, and Esau returned from the countryside exhausted. 30. Esau said to Jacob, 'Let me eat the red soup, that red soup there; I am exhausted'—hence the name given to him, Edom. 31. Jacob said, 'First sell me your birthright, then'. 32. Esau said, 'Here I am, at death's door; what use will my birthright be to me?' 33. Then Jacob said, 'First give me your oath'; he gave him his oath and sold his birthright to Jacob. 34. Then Jacob gave him bread and lentil soup, and after eating and drinking he got up and went. That was all Esau cared for his birthright.

ISAAC AND REBEKAH GO TO GERAR

 CHAPTER 26. 1. There was a famine in the land—a second one after the famine which took place in the time of Abraham—and Isaac went to Abimelech, the Philistine king at Gerar. 2. Yahweh appeared to him and said, 'Do not go down into Egypt; stay in the land I shall tell you of. 3. Remain for the present here in this land, and I will be with you and bless you. For it is to you and your descendants that I will give all these lands, and I will fulfil the oath I swore to your father Abraham. 4. I will make your descendants as many as the stars of heaven, and I will give them all these lands; and all the nations in the world shall bless themselves by your descendants 5. in return for Abraham's obedience; for he kept my charge, my commandments, my statutes and my laws.'

ISAAC'S FEAR FOR REBEKAH

6. So Isaac stayed at Gerar. 7. When the people of the place asked him about his wife he replied, 'She is my sister', for he was afraid to say, 'She is my wife', in case they killed him on Rebekah's account, for she was beautiful.

ABIMELECH DISCOVERS ISAAC'S DECEIT

8. When he had been there some time, Abimelech the Philistine king happened to look out of the window and saw Isaac fondling his wife Rebekah. 9. Abimelech summoned Isaac and said to him, 'Surely she must be your wife! How could you say she was your sister?' Isaac answered him, 'Because I thought I might be killed on her account'. 10. Abimelech said, 'What is this you have done to us? One of my subjects might easily have slept with your wife, and then you would have made us incur guilt.'

ABIMELECH PROTECTS ISAAC

11. Then Abimelech issued this order to all the people: 'Whoever touches this man or his wife shall be put to death'. 12. Isaac sowed his crops in that land, and that year he reaped a hundredfold. Yahweh blessed him 13. and the man became rich; he prospered more and more until he was very rich indeed. 14. He had flocks and herds and many servants. The Philistines began to envy him.

THE FOUNDERS OF BEER-SHEBA

15. The Philistines had sealed all the wells dug by his father's servants, filling them with earth. These had existed from the time of his father Abraham. 16. Abimelech said to Isaac, 'Leave us, for you have become much more powerful than we are'. 17. So Isaac left; he pitched camp in the Valley of Gerar and there he stayed. 18. Isaac dug again the wells made by the servants of his father Abraham and sealed by the Philistines after Abraham's death, and he gave them the same names as his father had given them. 19. Isaac's servants dug in the valley and found a well of spring-water.

20. But the shepherds of Gerar quarrelled with Isaac's shepherds, saying, 'That water is ours!' So Isaac named the well Esek, because they had quarrelled with him. 21. They dug another well, and there was a quarrel about that one too; so he named it Sitnah. 22. Then he left there, and dug another well, and since there was no quarrel about this one, he named it Rehoboth, saying, 'Now Yahweh has made room for us, so that we may thrive in the land'. 23.

From there he went up to Beersheba. 24. Yahweh appeared to him that night and said: 'I am the God of your father Abraham. Do not be afraid, for I am with you. I will bless you and make your descendants many in number on account of my servant Abraham.' 25. There he built an altar and invoked the name of Yahweh. There he pitched his tent, and there Isaac's servants sank a well. 26. Abimelech came from Gerar to see him, with his adviser Ahuzzath and the commander of his army, Phicol. 27. Isaac said to them, 'Why do you come to me since you hate me, and have made me leave you?' 28. 'It became clear to us that Yahweh was with you:' they replied 'and so we said, "Let there be a sworn treaty between ourselves and you, and let us make a covenant with you". 29. Swear not to do us any harm, since we never molested you but were unfailingly kind to you and let you go away in peace. Now you have Yahweh's blessing.' 30. He then made them a feast and they ate and drank. 31. Rising early in the morning, they exchanged oaths. Then Isaac bade them farewell and they went from him in peace. 32. Now it was on the same day that Isaac's servants brought him news of the well they had dug. 'We have found water!' they said to him. 33. So he called the well Sheba, and hence the town is named Beersheba to this day.

THE WIVES OF ESAU

34. When Esau was forty years old he married Judith,
the daughter of Beeri the Hittite, and Basemach, the
daughter of Elon the Hittite.

ISAAC'S DISAPPOINTMENT

35. These were a bitter disappointment to Isaac and
Rebekah.

ISAAC SEEKS TO BLESS ESAU

⌒⋎⋎⌒ CHAPTER 27. 1. Isaac had grown old, and his eyes were so weak that he could no longer see. He summoned his elder son Esau, 'My son!' he said to him, and the latter answered, 'I am here'. 2. Then he said, 'See, I am old and do not know when I may die. 3. Now take your weapons, your quiver and bow; go out into the country and hunt me some game. 4. Make me the kind of savoury I like and bring it to me, so that I may eat, and give you my blessing before I die.' 5. Rebekah happened to be listening while Isaac was talking to his son Esau. So when Esau went into the country to hunt game for his father, 6. Rebekah said to her son Jacob, 'I have just heard your father saying to your brother Esau, 7. "Bring me some game and make a savoury for me. Then I shall eat, and bless you in the presence of Yahweh before I die." 8. Now my son, listen to me and do as I tell you. 9. Go to the flock, and bring me back two good kids, so that I can make the kind of savoury your father likes. 10. Then you can take it to your father for him to eat so that he may bless you before he dies.' 11.

Jacob said to his mother Rebekah, 'Look, my brother Esau is hairy, while I am smooth-skinned. 12. If my father happens to touch me, he will see I am cheating him, and I shall bring down a curse on myself instead of a blessing.' 13. But his mother answered him, 'On me be the curse, my son! Just listen to me; go and fetch me the kids.' 14. So he went to fetch them, and he brought them to his mother, and she made the kind of savoury his father liked. 15. Rebekah took her elder son Esau's best clothes, which she had in the house, and dressed her younger son Jacob in them, 16. covering his arms and the smooth part of his neck with the skins of the kids.

JACOB STEALS HIS FATHER'S BLESSING

17. Then she handed the savoury and the bread she had made to her son Jacob. 18. He presented himself before his father and said, 'Father'. 'I am here;' was the reply 'who are you, my son?' 19. Jacob said to his father, 'I am Esau your first-born; I have done as you told me. Please get up and take your place and eat the game I have brought and then give me your blessing.' 20. Isaac said to his son, 'How quickly you found it, my son!' 'It was Yahweh your God' he answered 'who put it in my path.' 21. Isaac said to Jacob, 'Come here, then, and let me touch you, my son, to know if you are my son Esau or not'. 22. Jacob came close to his father Isaac, who touched him and said, 'The voice is Jacob's voice but the arms are the arms of Esau!' 23. He did not recognise him, for his arms were hairy like his brother Esau's, and so he blessed him. 24. He said, 'Are you really my son Esau?' And he replied, 'I am'. 25. Isaac said, 'Bring it here that I may eat the game my son has brought, and so may give you my blessing'. He brought it to him and he ate; he offered him wine, and he drank.

26. His father Isaac said to him, 'Come closer, and kiss me, my son'. 27. He went closer and kissed his father, who smelled the smell of his clothes. He blessed him saying: 'Yes, the smell of my son is like the smell of a fertile field blessed by Yahweh. 28. May God give you dew from heaven, and the richness of the earth, abundance of grain and wine! 29. May nations serve you and peoples bow down before you! Be master of your brothers; may the sons of your mother bow down before you! Cursed be he who curses you; blessed be he who blesses you!' 30. As soon as Isaac had finished blessing Jacob, and just when Jacob was leaving the presence of his father Isaac, his brother Esau returned from hunting. 31. He too made a savoury and brought it to his father. He said to him, 'Father, get up and eat the game your son has brought and then give me your blessing!'

THE REJECTION OF ESAU

32. His father Isaac asked him, 'Who are you?' 'I am
your firstborn son, Esau' he replied. 33. At this Isaac
was seized with a great trembling and said, 'Who was
it, then, that went hunting and brought me game?
Unsuspecting I ate before you came; I blessed him,
and blessed he will remain!' 34. When Esau heard
his father's words, he cried out loudly and bitterly to
his father, 'Father, bless me too!' 35. But he replied,
'Your brother came by fraud and took your blessing'.
36. Esau said, 'Is it because his name is Jacob, that
he has now supplanted me twice? First he took my
birthright, and look, now he has taken my blessing!
But' he added 'have you not kept a blessing for me?'
37. Isaac answered Esau, 'See, I have made him your
master; I have given him all his brothers as servants,
I have provided him with grain and wine. What can
I do for you, my son?' 38. Esau said to his father,
'Was that your only blessing, father? Father, give me
a blessing too.' Isaac remained silent, and Esau burst
into tears. 39. Then his father Isaac gave him this
answer: 'Far from the richness of the earth shall be

your dwelling-place, far from the dew that falls from heaven. 40. You shall live by your sword, and you shall serve your brother. But when you win your freedom, you shall shake his yoke from your neck.'

ESAU MEDITATES REVENGE

41. Esau hated Jacob because of the blessing his
father had given him, and thought thus to himself,
'The time to mourn for my father will soon be here.
Then I will kill my brother Jacob.' 42. When the
words of Esau, her elder son, were repeated to
Rebekah, she sent for her younger son Jacob and said
to him, 'Look, your brother Esau means to take
revenge and kill you.

JACOB FLEES TO HARAN

43. 'Now, my son, listen to me; go away and take refuge with my brother Laban in Haran. 44. Stay with him a while, until your brother's fury cools, 45. until your brother's anger against you cools and he forgets what you have done to him. Then I will send someone to bring you back. Why should I lose you both on the same day?' 46. Rebekah said to Isaac, 'I am tired to death because of the daughters of Heth. If Jacob marries one of the daughters of Heth like these, one of the women of the country, what meaning is there left in life for me?'

CHAPTER 28. 1. Isaac summoned Jacob and blessed him; and he gave him this order: 'You are not to choose a wife from the Canaanite women. 2. Away now to Paddan-aram, the home of Bethuel, your mother's father, and there choose a wife for yourself among the daughters of Laban, your mother's brother. 3. May El Shaddai bless you; may he make you fruitful and make you multiply so that you become a group of nations. 4. May he grant you the blessing of Abraham, and your descendants after you, so that you may take possession of the land in which you live now, which God gave to Abraham.' 5. Isaac sent Jacob away, and Jacob went to Paddan-aram, to Laban the son of Bethuel, the Aramaean, and brother of Rebekah, the mother of Jacob and Esau. 6. Esau saw that Isaac had blessed Jacob and sent him to Paddan-aram to choose a wife there, and that in blessing him he had given him this order: 'You are not to choose a wife from the Canaanite women', 7. and that in obedience to his father and mother Jacob had gone to Paddan-aram. 8. Esau saw from this that the women of Canaan were not held in favour by his father Isaac, 9. so he went to Ishmael and chose for wife, in addition to the wives he had, Mahalath, daughter of Abraham's son Ishmael and sister of Nebaioth.

JACOB'S DREAM

10. Jacob left Beersheba and set out for Haran. 11. When he had reached a certain place he passed the night there, since the sun had set. Taking one of the stones to be found at that place, he made it his pillow and lay down where he was. 12. He had a dream: a ladder was there, standing on the ground with its top reaching to heaven; and there were angels of God going up it and coming down. 13. And Yahweh was there, standing over him, saying, 'I am Yahweh, the God of Abraham your father, and the God of Isaac. I will give to you and your descendants the land on which you are lying. 14. Your descendants shall be like the specks of dust on the ground; you shall spread to the west and the east, to the north and the south, and all the tribes of the earth shall bless themselves by you and your descendants. 15. Be sure that I am with you; I will keep you safe wherever you go, and bring you back to this land, for I will not desert you before I have done all that I have promised you.' 16. Then Jacob awoke from his sleep and said, 'Truly, Yahweh is in this place and I never knew it!' 17. He

was afraid and said, 'How awe-inspiring this place is! This is nothing less than a house of God; this is the gate of heaven!'

JACOB'S PLEDGE TO YAHWEH

18. Rising early in the morning, Jacob took the stone he had used for his pillow, and set it up as a monument, pouring oil over the top of it. 19. He named the place Bethel, but before that the town was called Luz. 20. Jacob made this vow, 'If God goes with me and keeps me safe on this journey I am making, if he gives me bread to eat and clothes to wear, 21. and if I return home safely to my father, then Yahweh shall be my God. 22. This stone I have set up as a monument shall be a house of God, and I will surely pay you a tenth part of all you give me.'

JACOB MEETS RACHEL

CHAPTER 29.   1. Moving on, Jacob went to the land of the sons of the East. 2. He looked and there in the fields was a well with three flocks of sheep lying beside it, for this well was used for watering the flocks. Now the stone on the mouth of the well was a large one; 3. so they used to gather all the flocks there, and then roll the stone off the mouth of the well, to water the sheep; then they put the stone back in its place over the mouth of the well. 4. Jacob said to the shepherds, 'Brothers, where are you from?' They replied, 'We are from Haran'. 5. Then he asked them, 'Do you know Laban, the son of Nahor?' 'We know him' they replied. 6. Then he asked them, 'Does all go well with him?' 'Yes,' they replied 'and here comes his daughter Rachel with the sheep.' 7. Then he said, 'See, it is still broad daylight; it is not yet time to bring the animals in. Water the sheep and go and take them back to pasture.' 8. But they answered, 'We cannot do that until all the flocks are gathered and they roll the stone off the mouth of the well; then we shall water the sheep'. 9. He was still talking to them, when Rachel came with the sheep belonging to her father, for she was a shepherdess. 10. As soon as Jacob saw Rachel, the daughter of his uncle Laban, and the sheep of his uncle Laban, he came up and, rolling the stone off the mouth of the well, he watered the sheep of his uncle Laban.

JACOB WORKS TO WIN RACHEL

11. Jacob kissed Rachel and burst into tears. 12. He told Rachel he was her father's kinsman and Rebekah's son, and she ran to tell her father. 13. As soon as he heard her speak of his sister's son Jacob, Laban ran to meet him; and embracing him he kissed him warmly, and brought him to his house. Jacob told Laban every thing that had happened, 14. and Laban said to him, 'Truly you are my bone and flesh!' And Jacob stayed with him for a month. 15. Laban said to Jacob, 'Because you are my kinsman, are you to work for me without payment? Tell me what wages you want.' 16. Now Laban had two daughters, the elder named Leah, and the younger Rachel. 17. There was no sparkle in Leah's eyes, but Rachel was shapely and beautiful, 18. and Jacob had fallen in love with Rachel. So his answer was, 'I will work for you seven years to win your younger daughter Rachel'. 19. Laban replied, 'It is better for me to give her to you than to a stranger; stay with me'. 20. To win Rachel, therefore, Jacob worked seven years, and they seemed to him like a few days because he loved her so much.

21. Then Jacob said to Laban, 'Give me my wife, for my time is finished, and I should like to go to her'. 22. Laban gathered all the people of the place together, and gave a banquet. 23. But when night came he took his daughter Leah and brought her to Jacob, and he slept with her. 24. (Laban gave his slave-girl Zilpah to be his daughter Leah's slave.)

JACOB MARRIES LEAH, AND RACHEL

25. When morning came, there was Leah. So Jacob said to Laban, 'What is this you have done to me? Did I not work for you to win Rachel? Why then have you tricked me?' 26. Laban answered, 'It is not the custom in our country to give the younger before the elder. 27. Finish this marriage week and I will give you the other one too in return for your working with me another seven years.' 28. Jacob did this, and when the week was over, Laban gave him his daughter Rachel as his wife. 29. (Laban gave his daughter Rachel his slave-girl Bilhah to be her slave.) 30. So Jacob slept with Rachel also, and he loved Rachel more than Leah. He worked with Laban another seven years. 31. Yahweh saw that Leah was neglected, so he opened her womb, while Rachel remained barren. 32. Leah conceived and gave birth to a son whom she named Reuben, 'Because' she said 'Yahweh has seen my misery; now my husband will love me'. 33. Again she conceived and gave birth to a son, saying, 'Yahweh has heard that I was neglected, so he has given me this one too'; and she named him Simeon.

34. Again she conceived and gave birth to a son, saying, 'This time my husband will be united to me, for I have now borne three sons to him'; accordingly, she named him Levi. 35. Again she conceived and gave birth to a son, saying, 'This time I will give glory to Yahweh'; accordingly she named him Judah. Then she had no more children.

CHAPTER 30. 1. Rachel, seeing that she herself gave Jacob no children, became jealous of her sister. And she said to Jacob, 'Give me children, or I shall die!' 2. This made Jacob angry with Rachel, and he retorted, 'Am I in God's place? It is he who has refused you motherhood.' 3. So she said, 'Here is my slave-girl, Bilhah. Sleep with her so that she may give birth on my knees; through her, then, I too shall have children!' 4. So she gave him her slave-girl Bilhah as a wife. Jacob slept with her, 5. and Bilhah conceived and gave birth to a son by Jacob. 6. Then Rachel said, 'God has done me justice; yes, he has heard my prayer and given me a son'. Accordingly she named him Dan. 7. Again Rachel's slave-girl Bilhah conceived and gave birth to a second son by Jacob. 8. Then Rachel said, 'I have fought God's fight with my sister, and I have won'; so she named him Naphtali. 9. Now Leah, seeing that she had no more children, took her slave-girl Zilpah and gave her to Jacob as a wife. 10. So Leah's slave-girl Zilpah gave birth to a son by Jacob. 11. Then Leah exclaimed, 'What good fortune!' So she named him Gad. 12. Leah's slave-girl Zilpah gave birth to a second son by Jacob. 13. Then Leah said, 'What happiness! Women will call me happy!' So she named him Asher. 14. Going out when they were harvesting the corn, Reuben found some mandrakes and brought them to his mother Leah. Rachel said to Leah, 'Please give me some of your son's mandrakes'. 15. But Leah replied, 'Is it not enough to have taken my husband that you should want to take my son's mandrakes too?' So Rachel said, 'Very well, he shall sleep with you to-night in return for your son's mandrakes'. 16. When Jacob came back from the fields that night, Leah went out to meet him, saying, 'You must come to me, for I have hired you at the price of my son's mandrakes'. So he slept with her that night. 17. God heard Leah, and she conceived and gave birth to a fifth son by Jacob. 18. Then Leah said, 'God has paid me my wages for giving my slave-girl to my husband'. So she named him Issachar. 19. Again Leah conceived and gave birth to a sixth son by Jacob, 20. saying, 'God has given me a fine gift; now my husband will honour me, for I have borne six children to him'. So she named him Zebulun. 21. Later she gave birth to a daughter and named her Dinah. 22. Then God remembered Rachel; he heard her and opened her womb. 23. She conceived and gave birth to a son, saying, 'God has taken away my shame'. 24. So she named him Joseph, saying, 'May Yahweh give me another son!'

JACOB TRICKS LABAN

25. When Rachel had given birth to Joseph, Jacob said to Laban, 'Release me, and then I can go home to my own country. 26. Give me my wives for whom I have worked for you, and my children, so that I can go. You know very well the work I have done for you.' 27. Laban said to him, 'If I have won your friendship... I learned from the omens that Yahweh had blessed me on your account. 28. So name your wages,' he added 'and I will pay you.' 29. He answered him, 'You know very well how hard I have worked for you, and how your stock has fared in my charge. 30. The little you had before I came has increased enormously, and Yahweh has blessed you wherever I have been. But when am I to provide for my own House?' 31. Laban said, 'How much am I to pay you?' And Jacob replied, 'You will not have to pay me anything: if you do for me as I propose, I will be your shepherd once more and look after your flock. 32. Today I will go through all your flock. Take out of it every black animal among the sheep, and every speckled or spotted one among the goats. Such shall be my wages,

33. and my honesty will answer for me later: when you come to check my wages, every goat I have that is not speckled or spotted, and every sheep that is not black shall rank as stolen property in my possession.' 34. Laban replied, 'Good! Let it be as you say.' 35. That same day he took out the striped and speckled he-goats and all the spotted and speckled she-goats, every one that had white on it, and all the black sheep. He handed them over to his sons, 36. and put three days' journey between himself and Jacob. Jacob took care of the rest of Laban's flock. 37. Jacob gathered branches in sap, from poplar, almond and plane trees, and peeled them in white strips, laying bare the white on the branches. 38. He put the branches he had peeled in front of the animals, in the troughs in the channels where the animals came to drink; and the animals mated when they came to drink. 39. They mated therefore in front of the branches and so produced striped, spotted and speckled young. 40. As for the sheep, Jacob put them apart, and he turned the animals towards whatever was striped or black in Laban's flock. Thus he built up droves of his own which he did not put with Laban's flock. 41. Moreover, whenever the sturdy animals mated, Jacob put the branches where the animals could see them, in the troughs, so that they would mate in front of the branches. 42. But when the animals were feeble, he did not put them there; thus Laban got the feeble, and Jacob the sturdy, 43. and he grew extremely rich, and became the owner of large flocks, with men and women slaves, camels and donkeys.

JACOB RETURNS TO CANAAN

CHAPTER 31. 1. Jacob learned that the sons of Laban were saying, 'Jacob has taken everything that belonged to our father; it is at our father's expense that he has acquired all this wealth'. 2. Jacob saw from Laban's face that things were not as they had been. 3. Yahweh said to Jacob, 'Go back to the land of your forefathers and to your kindred; and I will be with you'. 4. So Jacob had Rachel and Leah called to the fields where his flocks were, 5. and he said to them, 'I can see from your father's face that I am out of favour with him now; but the God of my father has been with me. 6. You yourselves know that I have worked for your father with all my strength. 7. Your father has tricked me, ten times changing my wages, yet God has not allowed him to harm me. 8. Whenever he said, "The spotted ones shall be your wages", all the animals produced spotted young; whenever he said, "The striped ones shall be your wages", all the animals produced striped young. 9. Thus God has taken your father's livestock and given it to me. 10. It happened at the time when the animals were on heat, that in a dream I looked up and saw that the males covering the females of the flock were striped or spotted or piebald. 11. In the dream the angel of God called to me, "Jacob!" And I answered: I am here. 12. He said, "Look up and see: all the males covering the females of the flock are striped or spotted or piebald, for I have seen all that Laban has done to you. 13. I am the God of Bethel where you poured oil on a monument, and where you made a vow to me. Now get ready to leave this country and return to the land of your birth." ' 14. In answer Rachel and Leah said to him, 'Have we any share left in the inheritance of our father's House? 15. Does he not treat us as foreigners, for he has sold us and gone on to use up all our money? 16. Surely all the riches God has taken from our father belong to us and to our children. So do all that God has told you.' 17. Jacob made ready and put his children and his wives on camels, 18. and he drove all his livestock before him—with all he had acquired, the livestock belonging to him which he had acquired in Paddan-aram—to go to his father Isaac in the land of Canaan.

RACHEL STEALS HER FATHER'S IDOLS

19. When Laban had gone to shear his flock, Rachel stole the household idols belonging to her father. 20. Jacob outwitted Laban the Aramaean by giving him no inkling of his flight. 21. He fled with all he had and went away, crossing the River and making for Mount Gilead. 22. Three days later Laban was told that Jacob had fled. 23. Taking his brothers with him he pursued him for seven days and overtook him at Mount Gilead.

LABAN ACCUSES JACOB

24. God came by night in a dream to Laban the Aramaean and said to him, 'On no account say anything whatever to Jacob'. 25. Laban caught up with Jacob, who had pitched his tent in the hills; and Laban pitched camp on Mount Gilead. 26. Laban said to Jacob, 'What have you done, tricking me and driving my daughters off like prisoners of war? 27. Why did you flee in secret, stealing away without letting me know so that I could send you on your way rejoicing, with songs and the music of tambourines and lyres? 28. You did not even let me kiss my sons and daughters. You have behaved like a fool. 29. It is in my power to do you harm, but the God of your father said to me last night, "On no account say anything whatever to Jacob". 30. Now it may be you really went because you had such a longing for your father's House, but why did you steal my gods?' 31. Jacob answered Laban, 'I was afraid, thinking you were going to snatch your daughters from me. 32. But whoever is found in possession of your gods shall not remain alive. In the presence of our brothers, examine for

yourself what I have, and take what is yours.' Now Jacob did not know that Rachel had stolen them. 33. Laban went into Jacob's tent, and then into Leah's tent and the tent of the two slave-girls, but he found nothing. He came out of Leah's tent and went into Rachel's. 34. Now Rachel had taken the household idols and put them in the camel's litter, and was sitting on them. Laban went through everything in the tent but found nothing.

35. Then Rachel said to her father, 'Do not look angry, my lord, because I cannot rise in your presence, for I am as women are from time to time'. Laban searched but did not find the idols. 36. Then Jacob lost his temper and took Laban to task. And Jacob said to Laban, 'What is my offence, what is my crime, that you have set on me? 37. You have gone through all my belongings; have you found anything belonging to your House? Produce it here in the presence of my brothers and yours, and let them decide between the two of us. 38. In all the twenty years I have been with you, your ewes and your she-goats have never miscarried, and I have eaten none of the rams from your flock. 39. As for those mauled by wild beasts, I have never brought them back to you, but have borne the loss myself; you claimed them from me, whether I was robbed by day or robbed by night. 40. In the daytime the heat has consumed me, and at night the cold has gnawed at me, and sleep has fled from my eyes. 41. These twenty years I have been in your house; fourteen years I have worked for you for your two daughters, and six years for your flock; and ten times you have changed my wages. 42. If the God of my father, the God of Abraham, the Kinsman of Isaac, had not been with me, you would have sent me away empty-handed. But God has seen my weariness and the work done by my hands, and last night he delivered judgement.' 43. Laban gave Jacob this answer, 'These daughters are my daughters and these sons are my sons; these sheep are my sheep, and all that you see belongs to me. But what can I do today about my daughters, and about the sons they have borne? 44. Come now, let us make a covenant, you and I..., and let it serve as a witness between us.' 45. Then Jacob took a stone and set it up as a monument. 46. Jacob said to his kinsmen, 'Collect some

stones', and gathering some stones they made a cairn. They had a meal there, on the cairn, and 47. Laban called it Jegar-sahadutha while Jacob called it Galeed. 48. Laban said, 'May this cairn be a witness between us today'. That is why he named it Galeed, 49. and also Mizpah, because he said, 'Let Yahweh act as watchman between us when we are no longer in sight of each other. 50. If you ill-treat my daughters or marry other women in addition to my daughters, even though no one be with us, remember: God is witness between us.'

A BOUNDARY IS ESTABLISHED

51. Then Laban said to Jacob, 'Here is this cairn I have thrown up between us, and here is the monument. 52. This cairn is a witness, and the monument bears witness: I must not pass this cairn to attack you, and you must not pass this cairn and this monument to attack me. 53. May the God of Abraham and the god of Nahor judge between us.' Then Jacob swore by the Kinsman of his father Isaac. 54. He offered a sacrifice on the mountain and invited his brothers to the meal. They ate the meal, and passed the night on the mountain.

CHAPTER 32. 1. Laban rose early next morning, and kissing his sons and daughters he blessed them. Then Laban left to return home. 2. While Jacob was going on his way angels of God met him, 3. and on seeing them he said, 'This is God's camp', and he named the place Mahanaim. 4. Jacob sent messengers ahead of him to his brother Esau in the land of Seir, the countryside of Edom, 5. with these instructions, 'Say this to my lord Esau, "Here is the message of your servant Jacob: I have been staying with Laban till now, 6. and have acquired oxen, beasts of burden and flocks, and men and women slaves. I send news of this to my lord in the hope of winning your approval." 7. The messengers returned to Jacob and told him, 'We went to your brother Esau, and he is already on his way to meet you; there are four hundred men with him'. 8. Jacob was greatly afraid and distressed. He divided the people with him, and the flocks and cattle, into two companies, 9. saying, 'If Esau comes to one of the companies and attacks it, the other company will be left to escape'. 10. Jacob said, 'O God of my father Abraham, and God of my father Isaac, Yahweh who said to me, "Go back to your country and family, and I will make you prosper", 11. I am unworthy of all the kindness and goodness you have shown your servant. I had only my staff when I crossed the Jordan here, and now I can form two companies. 12. I implore you, save me from my brother's clutches, for I am afraid of him; he may come and attack us and the mothers and their children. 13. Yet it was you who said, "I will make you prosper, and make your descendants like the sand on the seashore, so many that it cannot be counted".' 14. Then Jacob passed that night there. From what he had with him he chose a gift for his brother Esau: 15. two hundred she-goats and twenty he-goats, two hundred ewes and twenty rams, 16. thirty camels in milk with their calves, forty cows and ten bulls, twenty she-asses and ten donkeys. 17. He put them in the charge of his servants, in separate droves, and he told his servants, 'Go ahead of me, leaving a space between each drove and the next'. 18. He gave the first this order: 'When my brother Esau meets you and asks, "To whom do you belong? Where are you going? Whose are those animals that you are driving?" 19. you will answer, "To your servant Jacob. They are a gift sent to my lord Esau. Jacob himself is following." ' 20. He gave the same order to the second and the third, and to all who were following the droves, 'That is what you must say to Esau when you find him. 21. You must say, "Yes, your servant Jacob himself is following".' For he argued, 'I shall conciliate him by sending a gift in advance; so when I come face to face with him he may perhaps receive me favourably'. 22. The gift went ahead of him, but he himself spent that night in the camp.

JACOB WRESTLES ALL NIGHT

23. That same night he rose, and taking his two wives and his two slave-girls and his eleven children he crossed the ford of the Jabbok. 24. He took them and sent them across the stream and sent all his possessions over too. 25. And Jacob was left alone. And there was one that wrestled with him until daybreak 26. who, seeing that he could not master him, struck him in the socket of his hip, and Jacob's hip was dislocated as he wrestled with him. 27. He said, 'Let me go, for day is breaking'. But Jacob answered, 'I will not let you go unless you bless me'. 28. He then asked, 'What is your name?' 'Jacob', he replied. 29. He said, 'Your name shall no longer be Jacob, but Israel, because you have been strong against God, you shall prevail against men'. 30. Jacob then made this request, 'I beg you, tell me your name', but he replied, 'Why do you ask my name?' And he blessed him there. 31. Jacob named the place Peniel, 'Because I have seen God face to face,' he said 'and I have survived'. 32. The sun rose as he left Peniel, limping because of his hip. 33. That is the reason why to this

day the Israelites do not eat the sciatic nerve which is in the socket of the hip; because he had struck Jacob in the socket of the hip on the sciatic nerve.

JACOB MEETS ESAU

CHAPTER 33. 1. Looking up Jacob saw Esau arriving with four hundred men. Accordingly he divided the children between Leah, Rachel and the two slave-girls. 2. He put the slave-girls and their children in front, with Leah and her children following, and Rachel and Joseph behind. 3. He himself went ahead of them and bowed to the ground seven times before going up to his brother. 4. But Esau ran to meet him, took him in his arms and held him close and wept. 5. Then looking up he saw the women and children. 'Who are these with you?' he asked. Jacob answered, 'The children whom God has bestowed on your servant'. 6. The slave-girls then came up with their children, and they all bowed low. 7. Leah also came up along with her children, and they all bowed low. Finally Rachel and Joseph came up and bowed low. 8. Esau asked, 'What was the meaning of all the company that I have met?' 'It is to win my lord's favour' he replied. 9. 'Brother, I have plenty,' Esau answered 'keep what is yours.' 10. Jacob protested, 'Please, if I have found favour with you, accept the gift I offer. To speak truly, I came into your presence as into the presence of God, but you have received me kindly. 11. So accept the gift I have brought for you; since God has been generous to me, I have all I need.' And he urged him, and Esau accepted. 12. Esau said, 'Let us break camp and move off; I will lead you'. 13. But Jacob replied, 'My lord is aware that the children are weak, and that I must consider the sheep and the cows that have calved. If they are driven too hard, even for one day, the whole drove will die. 14. May it please my lord to go on ahead of his servant. For my part, I will move at a slower pace, to suit the flock I am driving and the children, until I join my lord in Seir.' 15. Then Esau said, 'But I must at least leave you some of the people accompanying me'. 'Why?' Jacob asked 'All I desire is to win your favour.' 16. So that day Esau resumed his journey to Seir.

DINAH

17. But Jacob left for Succoth, where he built himself
a house and made shelter for his livestock; that is
why the place was given the name of Succoth. 18.
Jacob arrived safely at the town of Shechem in
Canaanite territory, on his return from Paddan-
aram. He encamped opposite the town 19. and for
one hundred pieces of silver he bought from the sons
of Hamor, the father of Shechem, the piece of land
on which he had pitched his tent. 20. Here he erected
an altar which he called, 'El, God of Israel'.

CHAPTER 34. 1. Dinah, who was Jacob's
daughter by Leah, went out to visit the women of
that region.

SHECHEM INSULTS ISRAEL

2. Shechem, the son of Hamor the Hivite, who was ruler of that region, saw her, carried her off and raped her, and so dishonoured her. 3. But he was captivated by Dinah, the daughter of Jacob; he fell in love with the young girl and comforted her. 4. Accordingly Shechem said to his father Hamor, 'Get me this young girl, I want to marry her'. 5. Meanwhile, Jacob had heard how his daughter Dinah had been dishonoured, but since his sons were out in the country-side with his livestock, Jacob said nothing until they came back. 6. Hamor the father of Shechem went out to talk to Jacob. 7. When Jacob's sons returned from the countryside and heard the news, these men were outraged and infuriated that Shechem had insulted Israel by raping Jacob's daughter—an offence that could not be overlooked. 8. Hamor said to them, 'The heart of my son Shechem is set on your daughter; I beg you, let him marry her. 9. Ally yourselves with us by marriage; give us your daughters and take our daughters for yourselves. 10. Stay with us and the land shall be open to you to live in or move

through or own.' 11. Shechem said to the father and brothers of the young girl, 'If only I can win your favour, I will give you whatever you ask. 12. Demand from me a huge bridal price and gifts; I will give you as much as you ask. Only let me marry the young girl.' 13. Then came the answer Jacob's sons gave to Shechem and his father Hamor, a crafty answer because he had dishonoured their sister Dinah. 14. 'We cannot do such a thing' they said to them. 'To give our sister to an uncircumcised man would be a disgrace for us. 15. We can agree only on one condition: that you become like us by circumcising all your males. 16. Then we will give you our daughters, taking yours for ourselves; and we will stay with you to make one nation. 17. But if you do not listen to us on this matter of circumcision we shall take our daughter and go.' 18. Hamor and Shechem, Hamor's son, were pleased with what they heard. 19. The young man did not hesitate about doing this, for he was deeply in love with Jacob's daughter. Moreover he was the most important person in his fathers household. 20. Hamor and his son Shechem went to the gate of their town and spoke to their fellow townsmen saying, 21. 'These men are friendly; let them stay with us in the land, and move about as freely as they like. Let us marry their daughters and give our daughters to them. 22. But these men will agree to stay with us and become a single nation only on this condition: all males must be circumcised as they are. 23. Will not their livestock, their goods and all their cattle belong to us, if only we agree to let them stay with us?' 24. All the citizens of the town agreed to the proposal made by Hamor and his son Shechem, and so all the males were circumcised.

REVENGE BY TREACHERY

25. Now on the third day, when they were still in pain, Jacob's two sons Simeon and Levi, brothers of Dinah, took their swords and marched into the town unsuspected; they killed all the males. 26. They put Hamor and his son Shechem to the sword, took Dinah from Shechem's house and came away. 27. Jacob's sons attacked the wounded and pillaged the town because their sister had been dishonoured. 28. They took away their flocks, cattle, donkeys and whatever there was in the town and in the countryside. 29. They carried off all their riches, all their little children and their wives, and looted everything to be found in their houses. 30. Jacob said to Simeon and Levi, 'You have done me harm, putting me in bad odour with the people of this land, the Canaanites and the Perrizites. I have few men, whereas they will unite against me to defeat me and destroy me and my family.' 31. They retorted, 'Is our sister to be treated like a whore?'

CHAPTER 35. 1. God said to Jacob, 'Move on

now and go to Bethel and settle there. Make an altar there for the God who appeared to you when you were fleeing from your brother Esau.' 2. Jacob said to his family and to all who were with him, 'Get rid of the foreign gods you have with you; wash, and change your clothes. 3. We must move on and go to Bethel. There I will make an altar for the God who heard me when I was in distress, and gave me his help on the journey I made.' 4. They gave Jacob all the foreign gods in their possession, and the earrings that they were wearing. Jacob buried them under the oak tree near Shechem. 5. They broke camp; a divine terror struck the towns round about, and no one pursued the sons of Jacob. 6. When Jacob arrived at Luz in the land of Canaan—Bethel, in other words—and all the people with him, 7. he built an altar there, giving the place the name Bethel, because it was there that God had appeared to him when he was fleeing from his brother. 8. Deborah, who had been Rebekah's nurse, died and was buried below Bethel, under the oak tree; so they named it the Oak of Tears. 9. Once more God appeared to Jacob on his return from Paddan-aram, and blessed him. 10. God said to him, 'Your name is Jacob, but from now on you shall be named not Jacob but Israel'. Accordingly they named him Israel. 11. God said to him, 'I am El Shaddai. Be fruitful and multiply. A nation, indeed a group of nations shall descend from you. Even kings shall be numbered among your descendants. 12. I give you this land, the land I gave to Abraham and to Isaac; and I will give this land to your descendants after you.' 13. Then God went up from him. 14. Jacob raised a monument in the place where he had spoken with him, a stone monument, on which he made a libation and poured oil. 15. Jacob named the place Bethel where God had spoken with him.

THE DEATH OF RACHEL

16. They left Bethel, and while they were still some distance from Ephrath, Rachel began to be in labour, and her pains were severe. 17. But in her difficult delivery the midwife said to her, 'Do not be afraid; you have another son here'. 18. At the moment when she breathed her last, for she was dying, she named him Ben-oni. His father however named him Benjamin.

RACHEL'S TOMB AT BETHLEHEM

19. So Rachel died and was buried on the road to Ephrath, at Bethlehem. 20. Jacob raised a monument on her grave, and this is the monument of the tomb of Rachel which is still there today. 21. Israel left and pitched his tent beyond Migdal-eder. 22. While Israel was living in that district, Reuben went and slept with Bilhah his father's concubine, and Israel learned of it. Jacob's sons numbered twelve. 23. The sons of Leah: Jacob's eldest son Reuben, then Simeon, Levi, Judah, Issachar and Zebulim. 24. The sons of Rachel: Joseph and Benjamin. 25. The sons of Bilhah, Rachel's slave-girl: Dan and Naphtali. 26. The sons of Zilpah, Leah's slave-girl: Gad and Asher. These are the sons born to Jacob in Paddan-aram. 27. Jacob reached the house of his father Isaac at Mamre, at Kiriath-arba—or Hebron—where Abraham and Isaac had stayed. 28. Isaac was one hundred and eighty years old 29. when he breathed his last. He died and was gathered to his people, an old man who had enjoyed his full span of life. His sons Esau and Jacob buried him.

CHAPTER 36. 1. **Here** are the descendants of Esau, who is Edom. 2. Esau married women of Canaan: Adah, the daughter of Elon the Hittite, Oholibamah, the daughter of Anah, who was the son of Zibeon the Horite, 3. Basemath, the daughter of Ishmael and sister of Nebaioth. 4. Adah bore to Esau Eliphaz, Basemath bore Reuel, 5. Oholibamah bore Jeush, Jalam and Korah. These are the sons of Esau born to him in the land of Canaan. 6. Esau, taking his wives, his sons and daughters, all the members of his household, his livestock, all his cattle and all the goods he had acquired in the land of Canaan, left for the land of Seir away from his brother Jacob. 7. For they had acquired too much to live together. The land in which they were at that time could not support both because of their livestock. 8. That is why Edom settled in the mountainous region of Seir. Esau is Edom. 9. Here are the descendants of Esau, the father of Edom, in the mountainous region of Seir. 10. Here are the names of Esau's sons: Eliphaz the son of Adah, Esau's wife, and Reuel the son of Basemath, Esau's wife. 11. The sons of Eliphaz were: Teman, Omar, Zepho, Gatam, Kenaz. 12. Eliphaz son of Esau had Timna for concubine and and she bore him Amalek. These are the sons of Adah, Esau's wife. 13. Here are the sons of Reuel: Nahath, Zerah, Shammah, Mizzah. These are the sons of Basemath, Esau's wife. 14. Here are the sons of Esau's wife Oholibamah, daughter of Anah son of Zibeon: she bore him Jeush, Jalam and Korah. 15. Here are the chiefs of the sons of Esau. The sons of Eliphaz, first-born of Esau: chief Teman, chief Omar, chief Zepho, chief Kenaz, 16. chief Gatam, chief Amalek. These are the chiefs of Eliphaz in the land of Edom, these are the sons of Adah. 17. And here are the sons of Reuel son of Esau: chief Nahath, chief Zerah, chief Shammah, chief Mizzah. These are the chiefs of Reuel in the land of Edom, these are the sons of Basemath, Esau's wife. 18. And here are the sons of Oholibamah, Esau's wife: chief Jeush, chief Jalam, chief Korah. These are the chiefs of Esau's wife Oholibamah, daughter of Anah. 19. These are the sons of Esau and these are their chiefs. This is Edom. 20. Here are the sons of Seir the Horite, natives of the land: Lotan, Shobal, Zibeon, Anah, 21. Dishon,

Ezer, Dishan, these are the chiefs of the Horites, the sons of Seir in the land of Edom. 22. The sons of Lotan were Hori and Hemam, and Lotan's sister was Timna. 23. Here are the sons of Shobal: Alvan, Manahath, Ebal, Shepo, Onam. 24. Here are the sons of Zibeon: Aiah, Anah—the Anah who found the hot springs in the wilderness as he pastured the donkeys of his father Zibeon. 25. Here are the children of Anah: Dishon, Oholibamah daughter of Anah. 26. Here are the sons of Dishon: Hemdan, Eshban, Ithran, Cheran. 27. Here are the sons of Ezer: Bilhan, Zaavan, Akan. 28. Here are the sons of Dishan: Uz and Aran. 29. Here are the chiefs of the Horites: chief Lotan, chief Shobal, chief Zibeon, chief Anah, 30. chief Dishon, chief Ezer, chief Dishan. These are the chiefs of the Horites according to their clans in the land of Seir. 31. Here are the kings who ruled in the land of Edom before an Israelite king ruled. 32. In Edom there ruled Bela son of Beor; his city was called Dinhabah. 33. Bela died and Jobab son of Zerah, from Bozrah, succeeded. 34. Jobab died and Husham of the land of the Temanites succeeded. 35. Husham died and Hadad son of Bedad succeeded; he defeated the Midianites in the country of Moab, and his city was called Avith. 36. Hadad died and Samlah of Masrekah succeeded. 37. Samlah died and Shaul of Rehoboth-han-nahar succeeded. 38. Shaul died and Baal-hanan son of Achbor succeeded. 39. Baal-hanan died and Hadad succeeded; his city was called Pau; his wife's name was Mehetabel daughter of Matred, from Me-zahab. 40. Here are the names of the chiefs of Esau according to their clans and localities, by name: chief Timna, chief Alvah, chief Jetheth, 41. chief Oholibamah, chief Elah, chief Pinon, 42. chief Kenaz, chief Teman, chief Mibzar, 43. chief Magdiel, chief Iram. These are the chiefs of Edom according to their residence in the land that was theirs. This is Esau, father of Edom.

ISRAEL'S SON, JOSEPH

⁓ CHAPTER 37. 1. But Jacob lived in the land where his father had stayed, the land of Canaan. 2. This is the story of Joseph. Joseph was seventeen years old. As he was still young, he was shepherding the flock with his brothers, with the sons of Bilhah and Zilpah his father's wives. Joseph informed their father of the evil spoken about them. 3. Israel loved Joseph more than all his other sons, for he was the son of his old age, and he had a coat with long sleeves made for him. 4. But his brothers, seeing how his father loved him more than all his other sons, came to hate him so much that they could not say a civil word to him.

JOSEPH'S DREAM

5. Now Joseph had a dream, and he repeated it to his brothers. 6. 'Listen' he said 'to this dream I have had. 7. We were binding sheaves in the countryside; and my sheaf, it seemed, rose up and stood upright; then I saw your sheaves gather round and bow to my sheaf.' 8. 'So you want to be king over us,' his brothers retorted 'or to lord it over us?' And they hated him still more, on account of his dreams and of what he said.

ANOTHER DREAM

9. He had another dream which he told to his brothers. 'Look, I have had another dream' he said. 'I thought I saw the sun, the moon and eleven stars, bowing to me.' 10. He told his father and brothers, and his father scolded him. 'A fine dream to have!' he said to him. 'Are all of us then, myself, your mother and your brothers, to come and bow to the ground before you?' 11. His brothers were jealous of him, but his father kept the thing in mind. 12. His brothers went to pasture their father's flock at Shechem. 13. Then Israel said to Joseph, 'Are not your brothers with the flock at Shechem? Come, I am going to send you to them.' 'I am ready' he replied. 14. He said to him, 'Go and see how your brothers and the flock are doing, and bring me word'. He sent him from the valley of Hebron, and Joseph arrived at Shechem.

JOSEPH SEEKS HIS BROTHERS

15. A man found him wandering in the countryside
and the man asked him, 'What are you looking for?'
16. 'I am looking for my brothers' he replied. 'Please
tell me where they are pasturing their flock.' 17. The
man answered, 'They have moved on from here; indeed I heard them say, "Let us go to Dothan"'. So
Joseph went after his brothers and found them at
Dothan. 18. They saw him in the distance, and before
he reached them they made a plot among themselves
to put him to death. 19. 'Here comes the man of
dreams' they said to one another. 20. 'Come on, let
us kill him and throw him into some well; we can
say that a wild beast devoured him. Then we shall
see what becomes of his dreams.'

JOSEPH IS THROWN INTO A PIT

21. But Reuben heard, and he saved him from their violence. 'We must not take his life' he said. 22. 'Shed no blood,' said Reuben to them 'throw him into this well in the wilderness, but do not lay violent hands on him'—intending to save him from them and to restore him to his father. 23. So, when Joseph reached his brothers, they pulled off his coat, the coat with long sleeves that he was wearing, 24. and catching hold of him they threw him into the well, an empty well with no water in it.

THE PLOT AGAINST JOSEPH

25. They then sat down to eat. Looking up they saw a group of Ishmaelites who were coming from Gilead, their camels laden with gum, tragacanth, balsam and resin, which they were taking down into Egypt. 26. Then Judah said to his brothers, 'What do we gain by killing our brother and covering up his blood? 27. Come, let us sell him to the Ishmaelites, but let us not do any harm to him. After all, he is our brother, and our own flesh.' His brothers agreed.

JOSEPH IS SOLD INTO SLAVERY

28. Now some Midianite merchants were passing, and
they drew Joseph up out of the well. They sold Joseph
to the Ishmaelites for twenty silver pieces, and these
men took Joseph to Egypt.

REUBEN'S FEAR

29. When Reuben went back to the well there was no sign of Joseph. Tearing his clothes, 30. he went back to his brothers. 'The boy has disappeared' he said. 'What am I going to do?' 31. They took Joseph's coat and, slaughtering a goat, they dipped the coat in the blood.

JACOB'S SORROW

32. Then they sent back the coat with long sleeves and had it taken to their father, with the message, 'This is what we have found. Examine it and see whether or not it is your son's coat.' 33. He examined it and exclaimed, 'It is my son's coat! A wild beast has devoured him. Joseph has been the prey of some animal and has been torn to pieces.' 34. Jacob, tearing his clothes and putting on a loincloth of sackcloth, mourned his son for a long time. 35. All his sons and daughters came to comfort him, but he refused to be comforted. 'No,' he said 'I will go down in mourning to Sheol, beside my son.' And his father wept for him. 36. Meanwhile the Midianites had sold him in Egypt to Potiphar, one of Pharaoh's officials and commander of the guard.

CHAPTER 38. 1. It happened at that time that Judah left his brothers, to go down and stay with an Adullamite called Hirah. 2. There Judah saw the daughter of a Canaanite called Shua. He made her his wife and slept with her. 3. She conceived and gave birth to a son whom she named Er. 4. She conceived again and gave birth to a son whom she named Onan. 5. Yet again she gave birth to a son whom she named Shelah. She was at Chezib when she gave birth to him. 6. Judah took a wife for his first-born Er, and her name was Tamar. 7. But Er, Judah's first-born, offended Yahweh greatly, so Yahweh brought about his death. 8. Then Judah said to Onan, 'Take your brother's wife, and do your duty as her brother-in-law, to produce a child for your brother'. 9. But Onan, knowing the child would not be his, spilt his seed on the ground every time he slept with his brother's wife, to avoid providing a child for his brother. 10. What he did was offensive to Yahweh, so he brought about his death also. 11. Then Judah said to his daughter-in-law Tamar, 'Return home as a widow to your father, and wait for my son Shelah to grow up', for he was thinking, 'He must not die like his brothers'. So Tamar went back home to her father. 12. A long time passed, and then Shua's daughter, the wife of Judah, died. After Judah had been comforted he went up to Timnah to the men who sheared his sheep, himself and Hirah, his Adullamite friend. 13. This was reported to Tamar, 'Listen, your father-in-law is going up to Timnah for the shearing of his sheep'. 14. She therefore changed her widow's clothes, wrapped a veil around her, and sat down, heavily swathed, where the road to Enaim branches off the road to Timnah. Shelah had now grown up, as she saw, and yet she had not been given to him as his wife. 15. Judah, seeing her, took her for a prostitute, since her face was veiled. 16. Going up to her on the road, he said, 'Come, let me sleep with you'. He did not know that she was his daughter-in-law. 'What will you give me to sleep with me?' she asked. 17. 'I will send you a kid from the flock' he answered. 'Agreed, if you give me a pledge until you send it' she answered. 18. 'What pledge shall I give you?' he asked. 'Your seal, your cord and the stick you are holding' she answered. He gave them to her and slept with her and she conceived by him. 19. Then she rose and left him, and taking off her veil she put on her widow's weeds. 20. Judah sent the kid by his Adullamite friend to recover the pledge from the woman. But he did not find her. 21. He inquired from the men of the place, 'Where is the prostitute who was by the road-side at Enaim?' 'There has been no prostitute there', they answered. 22. So returning to Judah he said, 'I did not find her. What is more, the men of the place told me there had been no prostitute there.' 23. 'Let her keep what she has' Judah replied 'or we shall become a laughing-stock. At least I sent her this kid, even though you did not find her.' 24. About three months later it was reported to Judah, 'Your daughter-in-law has played the harlot; furthermore, she is pregnant, as a result of her misconduct'. 'Take her outside and burn her' said Judah. 25. But as she was being led off she sent this message to her father-in-law, 'It was the man to whom these things belong who made me pregnant. Look at them' she said 'and see whose seal and cord and stick these are.' 26. Judah examined them and then said, 'She is in the right, rather than I. This comes of my not giving her to my son Shelah to be his wife.' He had no further inter-course with her. 27. When the time for her con-finement came she was found to have twins in her womb. 28. During the delivery one of them put out a hand, and the midwife caught it and tied a scarlet thread to it, saying, 'This is the first to arrive'. 29. But he drew his hand back, and it was his brother who came out first. Then she said, 'What a breach you have opened for yourself!' So he was named Perez. 30. Then his brother came out with the scarlet thread on his hand, so he was named Zerah.

JOSEPH SERVES POTIPHAR

CHAPTER 39. 1. Now Joseph had been taken down into Egypt. Potiphar the Egyptian, one of Pharaoh's officials and commander of the guard, bought him from the Ishmaelites who had brought him down there. 2. Yahweh was with Joseph, and everything went well with him. He lodged in the house of his Egyptian master, 3. and when his master saw how Yahweh was with him and how Yahweh made everything succeed that he turned his hand to, 4. he was pleased with Joseph and made him his personal attendant; and his master put him in charge of his household, entrusting everything to him. 5. And from the time he put him in charge of his household and all his possessions, Yahweh blessed the Egyptian's household out of consideration for Joseph; Yahweh's blessing extended to all his possessions, both household and estate. 6. So he left Joseph to handle all his possessions, with and him at hand, concerned himself with nothing beyond the food he ate.

POTIPHAR'S WIFE

7. Now Joseph was well built and handsome, and it happened some time later that his master's wife looked desirously at him and said, 'Sleep with me'. 8. But he refused, and answered his master's wife, 'Because of me, my master does not concern himself with what happens in the house; he has handed over all his possessions to me. 9. He is no more master in this house than I am. He has withheld nothing from me except yourself, because you are his wife. How could I do anything so wicked, and sin against God?' 10. Although she spoke to Joseph day after day he would not agree to sleep with her and surrender to her.

AN UNJUST ACCUSATION

11. But one day Joseph in the course of his duties came to the house, and there was not a servant there indoors. 12. The woman caught hold of him by his tunic and said, 'Sleep with me'. But he left the tunic in her hand and ran out of the house. 13. Seeing he had left the tunic in her hand and left the house, 14. she called her servants and said to them, 'Look at this! He has brought us a Hebrew to insult us. He came to me to sleep with me, but I screamed, 15. and when he heard me scream and shout he left his tunic beside me and ran out of the house.' 16. She put the tunic down by her side until the master came home. 17. Then she told him the same tale, 'The Hebrew slave you bought us came to insult me. 18. But when I screamed and called out he left his garment by my side and made his escape.' 19. When the master heard his wife say, 'This is how your slave treated me', he was furious.

JOSEPH IN PRISON

20. Joseph's master had him arrested and committed to the gaol where the king's prisoners were kept. And there in gaol he stayed. 21. But Yahweh was with Joseph. He was kind to him and made him popular with the chief gaoler. 22. The chief gaoler put Joseph in charge of all the prisoners in the gaol, making him responsible for everything done there. 23. The chief gaoler did not need to interfere with Joseph's administration, for Yahweh was with him, and Yahweh made everything he undertook successful.

PHARAOH'S CUP-BEARER, AND BAKER

⟨∿⟩ CHAPTER 40. 1. It happened some time later that the king of Egypt's cup-bearer and his baker offended their master the king of Egypt. 2. Pharaoh was angry with his two officials, the chief cup-bearer and the chief baker, 3. and put them under arrest in the house of the commander of the guard, in the gaol where Joseph was a prisoner. 4. The commander of the guard assigned Joseph to them to attend to their wants, and they remained under arrest for some time. 5. Now both of them had dreams on the same night, each with its own meaning for the cup-bearer and the baker of the king of Egypt, who were prisoners in the gaol. 6. When Joseph came to them in the morning, he saw that they looked gloomy, 7. and he asked the two officials who were with him under arrest in his master's house, 'Why these black looks today?' 8. They answered him, 'We have had a dream, but there is no one to interpret it'. 'Are not interpretations God's business?' Joseph asked them. 'Come, tell me.' 9. So the chief cup-bearer described his dream to Joseph, telling him, 'In my dream I saw a vine in front of me. 10. On the vine were three branches; no sooner had it budded than it blossomed, and its clusters became ripe grapes. 11. I had Pharaoh's cup in my hand; I picked the grapes and squeezed them into Pharaoh's cup, and put the cup into Pharaoh's hand.' 12. 'Here is the interpretation of it' Joseph told him. 'The three branches are three days. 13. In another three days Pharaoh will release you and restore you to your place. Then you will hand Pharaoh his cup, as you did before, when you were his cup-bearer. 14. But be sure to remember me when things go well with you, and do me the kindness of reminding Pharaoh about me, to get me out of this house. 15. I was kidnapped from the land of the Hebrews in the first place, and even here I have done nothing to warrant imprisonment.'

THE CHIEF BAKER'S DREAM

16. The chief baker, seeing that the interpretation had
been favourable, said to Joseph, 'I too had a dream;
there were three trays of cakes on my head. 17. In the
top tray there were all kinds of Pharaoh's favourite
cakes, but the birds ate them off the tray on my head.'
18. Joseph gave him this answer, 'Here is the interpretation of it: the three trays are three days. 19. In
another three days Pharaoh will release you and hang
you on a gallows, and the birds will eat the flesh off
your bones.' 20. And so it happened; the third day
was Pharaoh's birthday and he gave a banquet for all
his officials, and he released the chief cup-bearer and
the chief baker in the presence of his officials. 21. The
chief cup-bearer he restored to his position as cup-
bearer, to hand Pharaoh his cup; 22. the chief baker
he hanged. It was as Joseph had said in his interpretation. 23. But the chief cup-bearer did not remember
Joseph: he forgot him.

PHARAOH'S DREAM

⌒〰⌒ CHAPTER 41. 1. Two years later it happened that Pharaoh had a dream: he was standing by the Nile, 2. and there, coming up from the Nile, were seven cows, sleek and fat, and they began to feed among the rushes. 3. And seven other cows, ugly and lean, came up from the Nile after them; and these went over and stood beside the other cows on the bank of the Nile. 4. The ugly and lean cows ate the seven sleek and fat cows. Then Pharaoh awoke. 5. He fell asleep and dreamed a second time: there, growing on one stalk, were seven ears of corn full and ripe. 6. And sprouting up after them came seven ears of corn, meagre and scorched by the east wind. 7. The scanty ears of corn swallowed the seven full and ripe ears of corn. Then Pharaoh awoke; it was a dream. 8. In the morning Pharaoh, feeling disturbed, had all the magicians and wise men of Egypt summoned to him. Pharaoh told them his dream, but no one could interpret it for Pharaoh. 9. Then the chief cup-bearer addressed Pharaoh, 'Today I must recall my offences. 10. Pharaoh was angry with his servants and put myself and the chief baker under arrest in the house of the commander of the guard. 11. We had a dream on the same night, he and I, and each man's dream had a meaning for himself. 12. There was a young Hebrew with us, one of the slaves belonging to the commander of the guard. We told our dreams to him and he interpreted them, giving each of us the interpretation of his dream. 13. It turned out just as he interpreted for us: I was restored to my place, but the other man was hanged.' 14. Then Pharaoh had Joseph summoned, and they hurried him from prison. He shaved and changed his clothes, and came into Pharaoh's presence. 15. Pharaoh said to Joseph, 'I have had a dream which no one can interpret. But I have heard it said of you that when you hear a dream you can interpret it.' 16. Joseph answered Pharaoh, 'I do not count. It is God who will give Pharaoh a favourable answer.' 17. So Pharaoh told Joseph, 'In my dream I was standing on the bank of the Nile. 18. And there were seven cows, fat and sleek, coming up out of the Nile, and they began to feed among the rushes. 19. And seven other cows came up after them, starved, ugly and lean; I have never seen such poor cows in all the land of Egypt. 20. The lean and ugly cows ate up the seven fat cows. 21. But when they had eaten them up, it was impossible to tell they had eaten them, for they remained as lean as before. Then I woke up. 22. And then again in my dream, there, growing on one stalk, were seven ears of corn, beautifully ripe; 23. but sprouting up after them came seven ears of corn, withered, meagre and scorched by the east wind. 24. The shrivelled ears of corn swallowed the seven ripe ears of corn. I told the magicians this, but no one could tell me the meaning.'

JOSEPH INTERPRETS THE DREAM

25. Joseph told Pharaoh, 'Pharaoh's dreams are one and the same: God has revealed to Pharaoh what he is going to do. 26. The seven fine cows are seven years and the seven ripe ears of corn are seven years; it is one and the same dream. 27. The seven gaunt and lean cows coming up after them are seven years, as are the seven shrivelled ears of corn scorched by the east wind: there will be seven years of famine. 28. It is as I have told Pharaoh: God has revealed to Pharaoh what he is going to do. 29. Seven years are coming, bringing great plenty to the whole land of Egypt, 30. but seven years of famine will follow them, when all the plenty in the land of Egypt will be forgotten, and famine will exhaust the land. 31. The famine that is to follow will be so very severe that no one will remember what plenty the country enjoyed. 32. The reason why the dream came to Pharaoh twice is because the event is already determined by God, and God is impatient to bring it about. 33. Pharaoh should now choose a man who is intelligent and wise to govern the land of Egypt. 34. Pharaoh should take

action and appoint supervisors over the land, and impose a tax of one-fifth on the land of Egypt during the seven years of plenty. 35. They will collect all food produced during these good years that are coming. They will store the corn in Pharaoh's name, and place the food in the towns and hold it there. 36. This food will serve as a reserve for the land during the seven years of famine that will afflict the land of Egypt. And so the land will not be destroyed by the famine.' 37. Pharaoh and all his ministers approved of what he had said.

JOSEPH BECOMES GOVERNOR OF EGYPT

38. Then Pharaoh asked his ministers, 'Can we find any other man like this, possessing the spirit of God?' 39. So Pharaoh said to Joseph, 'Seeing that God has given you knowledge of all this, there can be no one as intelligent and wise as you. 40. You shall be my chancellor, and all my people shall respect your orders; only this throne shall set me above you.' 41. Pharaoh said to Joseph, 'I hereby make you governor of the whole land of Egypt'. 42. Pharaoh took the ring from his hand and put it on Joseph's. He clothed him in fine linen and put a gold chain round his neck. 43. He made him ride in the best chariot he had after his own, and they cried before him 'Abrek'. This is the way he was made governor of the whole land of Egypt. 44. Pharaoh said to Joseph, 'I am Pharaoh: without your permission no one is to move hand or foot throughout the whole land of Egypt'. 45. Pharaoh named Joseph Zaphen-ath-paneah, and gave him Asenath the daughter of Potiphera, priest of On, for his wife. Joseph travelled through the land of Egypt.

PREPARATION FOR FAMINE

46. Joseph was thirty years old when he appeared before Pharaoh king of Egypt. After leaving Pharaoh's presence Joseph went through the whole land of Egypt. 47. During the seven years of plenty, the soil yielded generously. 48. He collected all the food of the seven years when there was an abundance in the land of Egypt, and allotted food to the towns, placing in each the food from the surrounding countryside. 49. Joseph stored the corn like the sand of the sea, so much that they stopped reckoning, since it was beyond all estimating. 50. Before the year of famine came, two sons were born to Joseph: Asenath, the daughter of Potiphera priest of On, bore him these. 51. Joseph named the first-born Manasseh, 'Because' he said 'God has made me forget all my suffering and all my father's household'. 52. He named the second Ephraim, 'Because' he said 'God has made me fruitful in the country of my misfortune'. 53. Then the seven years of plenty that there had been in the land of Egypt came to an end.

CORN IN EGYPT

54. The seven years of famine began to come as Joseph had said. There was famine in every country, but there was bread to be had throughout the land of Egypt. 55. When the whole country began to feel the famine, the people cried out to Pharaoh for bread. but Pharaoh told all the Egyptians, 'Go to Joseph and do what he tells you'.—56. There was famine all over the world.—Then Joseph opened all the granaries and sold grain to the Egyptians. The famine grew worse in the land of Egypt. 57. People came to Egypt from all over the world to buy grain from Joseph, for the famine had grown severe throughout the world.

JOSEPH'S BROTHERS SEEK FOOD

∽✺∽ CHAPTER 42. 1. Jacob, seeing that there was grain for sale in Egypt, said to his sons, 'Why do you stand looking at one another? 2. I hear' he said 'that there is grain for sale in Egypt. Go down and buy grain for us there, that we may survive and not die.' 3. So ten of Joseph's brothers went down to buy grain in Egypt. 4. But Jacob did not send Joseph's brother Benjamin with his brothers. 'Nothing must happen to him' he said. 5. Israel's sons with others making the same journey went to buy grain, for there was famine in the land of Canaan. 6. It was Joseph, as the man in authority over the country, who sold the grain to all comers. So Joseph's brothers went and bowed down before him, their faces touching the ground. 7. When Joseph saw his brothers he recognised them. But he did not make himself known to them, and he spoke harshly to them. 'Where have you come from?' he asked. 'From the land of Canaan to buy food' they replied. 8. So Joseph recognised his brothers, but they did not recognise him. 9. Joseph, remembering the dreams he had had about them, said to them,

'You are spies. You have come to discover the country's weak points.' 10. 'No, my lord,' they told him 'your servants have come to buy food. 11. We are all sons of the same man. We are honest men, your servants are not spies.' 12. 'Not so!' he replied 'It is the country's weak points you have come to discover.' 13. 'Your servants are twelve brothers,' they said 'sons of the same man, from the land of Canaan. The youngest, we should explain, is at present with our father, and the other one is no more.'

JOSEPH TESTS HIS BROTHERS

14. Joseph answered them, 'It is as I said, you are spies. 15. This is the test you are to undergo: as sure as Pharaoh lives you shall not leave unless your youngest brother comes here. 16. Send one of your number to fetch your brother; you others will remain under arrest, so that your statements can be tested to see whether or not you are honest. If not, then as sure as Pharaoh lives you are spies.' 17. Then he kept them all in custody for three days. 18. On the third day Joseph said to them, 'Do this and you shall keep your lives, for I am a man who fears God. 19. If you are honest men let one of your brothers be kept in the place of your detention; as for you, go and take grain to relieve the famine of your families. 20. You shall bring me your youngest brother; this way your words will be proved true, and you will not have to die!' This they did. 21. They said to one another,' 'Truly we are being called to account for our brother. We saw his misery of soul when he begged our mercy, but we did not listen to him and now this misery has come home to us.' 22. Reuben answered them, 'Did I not

tell you not to wrong the boy? But you did not listen, and now we are brought to account for his blood.' 23. They did not know that Joseph understood, because there was an interpreter between them.

JOSEPH HAS SIMEON BOUND

24. He left them and wept. Then he went back to them
and spoke to them. Of their number he took Simeon
and had him bound while they looked on. 25. Joseph
gave the order to fill their panniers with corn, to put
back each man's money in his sack, and to give them
provisions for the journey. This was done for them.
26. They loaded the grain on their donkeys and went
away. 27. But when they camped for the night one of
them opened his corn-sack to give fodder to his
donkey and saw his money in the mouth of his sack.
28. He said to his brothers, 'My money has been put
back; here it is in my corn-sack'. Their hearts sank,
and they looked at one another in panic, saying, 'What
is this that God has done to us?' 29. Returning to
their father Jacob in the land of Canaan, they gave
him a full report of what had happened to them,
30. 'The man who is lord of the land spoke harshly to
us, taking us for men spying on the country. 31. We
told him, "We are honest men, we are not spies. 32.
We are twelve brothers, sons of the same father. One
of us is no more, and the youngest is at present with

our father in the land of Canaan." 33. But the man who is lord of the land said to us, "This is how I shall know if you are honest: leave one of your brothers with me. Take the grain your families stand in need of, and go. 34. But bring me back your youngest brother and then I shall know that you are not spies but honest men. Then I will hand over your brother to you, and you can trade in the country." ' 35. As they emptied their sacks, each discovered his bag of money in his sack. On seeing their bags of money they were afraid, and so was their father. 36. Then their father Jacob said to them, 'You are robbing me of my children; Joseph is no more; Simeon is no more; and you now want to take Benjamin. All this I must bear.' 37. Then Reuben said to his father, 'You may put my two sons to death if I do not bring him back to you. Put him in my care and I will bring him back to you.' 38. But he replied, 'My son is not going down with you, for now his brother is dead he is the only one left. If any harm came to him on the journey you are to undertake, you would send me down to Sheol with my white head bowed in grief.'

ISRAEL SENDS BENJAMIN

⟨~⟩ CHAPTER 43. 1. But the country was hard-pressed by famine, 2. and when they had finished eating the grain they had brought from Egypt their father said to them, 'Go back and buy us a little food'. 3. 'But the man expressly warned us' Judah told him. He said, "You will not be admitted to my presence unless your brother is with you". 4. If you are ready to send our brother with us, we are willing to go down and buy food for you. 5. But if you are not ready to send him we will not go down, for the man told us, "You will not be admitted to my presence unless your brother is with you".' 6. Then Israel said,'Why did you bring this misery on me by telling the man you had another brother?' 7. They replied, 'He kept questioning us about ourselves and our kinsfolk, "Is your father still alive?" and, "Have you a brother?" That is why we told him. How could we know he was going to say, "Bring your brother down here"?' 8. Judah said to his father Israel, 'Send the boy with me. Let us start off and go, so that we may save our lives and not die, we, you, and our dependants. 9. I will go surety for him, and you can hold me responsible for him. If I do not bring him back to you and set him before you, let me bear the blame all my life. 10. Indeed, if we had not wasted so much time we should have been back again by now!' 11. Then their father Israel said to them, 'If it must be so, then do this: take some of the land's finest products in your panniers, and carry them down to the man as a gift, a little balsam, a little honey, gum, tragacanth, resin, pistachio nuts and almonds. 12. Take double the amount of money with you and return the money put back in the mouths of your sacks; it may have been a mistake. 13. Take your brother, and go back to the man. 14. May El Shaddai move the man to be kind to you, and you allow to bring back your other brother and Benjamin. As for me, if I must be bereaved, bereaved I must be.'

JOSEPH IS MOVED TO TEARS

15. The men took this gift; they took double the amount of money with them, and Benjamin. They started off and went down to Egypt. They presented themselves to Joseph. 16. When Joseph saw Benjamin with them he said to his chamberlain, 'Take these men to the house. Slaughter a beast and prepare it, for these men are to eat with me at midday.' 17. The man did as Joseph had ordered, and took the men to Joseph's house. 18. The men were afraid at being taken to Joseph's house, thinking, 'We are being taken there because of the money replaced in our corn-sacks the first time. They will set on us; they will fall on us and make slaves of us, and take our donkeys too.' 19. So they went up to Joseph's chamberlain and spoke to him at the entrance to the house. 20. 'By your leave, sir,' they said 'we came down once before to buy food, 21. and when we reached camp and opened our corn-sacks, there was each man's money in the mouth of his sack, to its full amount. But we have brought it back with us, 22. and we have brought more money with us to buy food. We do not know

who put our money in our corn-sacks.' 23. 'Peace to you,' he replied 'do not be afraid. Your God and your father's God has put a treasure in your corn-sacks. Your money reached me safely.' And he brought Simeon out to them. 24. The man took the men into Joseph's house. He offered them water to wash their feet, and gave their donkeys fodder. 25. They arranged their gift while they waited for Joseph to come at midday, for they had heard they were to dine there. 26. When Joseph arrived at the house they offered him the gift they had with them, and bowed before him to the ground. 27. But he greeted them kindly, asking, 'Is your father well, the old man you told me of? Is he still alive?' 28. 'Your servant our father is well,' they replied 'he is still alive', and they bowed low in homage. 29. Looking up he saw his brother Benjamin, his mother's son. 'Is this your youngest brother,' he asked 'of whom you told me?' Then he said to him, 'God be good to you, my son'. 30. Joseph hurried out, for his heart was moved at the sight of his brother and he was near to weeping. He went into his room and there he wept. 31. After bathing his face he returned and, controlling himself, gave the order: 'Serve the meal'. 32. He was served separately; so were they, and so were the Egyptians who ate in his household, for Egyptians cannot take food with Hebrews: they have a horror of it. 33. They were placed opposite him each according to his rank, from the eldest to the youngest, and the men looked at one another in amazement. 34. He had portions carried to them from his own dish, the portion for Benjamin being five times larger than any of the others. They drank with him and were happy.

THE CUP IN BENJAMIN'S SACK

CHAPTER 44. 1. Joseph gave this order to his chamberlain: 'Fill these men's sacks with as much food as they can carry, and put each man's money in the mouth of his sack. 2. And put my cup, the silver one, in the mouth of the youngest one's sack as well as the money for his grain.' He carried out the instructions Joseph had given. 3. When morning came and it was light, the men were sent off with their donkeys. 4. They had scarcely left the city, and had not gone far before Joseph said to his chamberlain, Away now and follow those men. When you catch up with them say to them, "Why did you reward good with evil? 5. Is this not the one my lord uses for drinking and also for reading omens? What you have done is wrong." ' 6. So when he caught up with them he repeated these words. 7. They asked him, 'What does my lord mean? Your servants would never think of doing such a thing. 8. Look, the money we found in the mouths of our corn-sacks we brought back to you from the land of Canaan. Are we likely to have stolen silver or gold from your master's house? 9.

Whichever of your servants is found to have it shall die, and we ourselves shall be slaves of my lord.' 10. 'Very well, then,' he replied 'it shall be as you say. The one on whom it is found shall become my slave, but the rest of you can go free.' 11. Each of them quickly lifted his corn-sack to the ground, and each opened his own. 12. He searched them, beginning with the eldest and ending with the youngest, and found the cup in Benjamin's sack. 13. Then they tore their clothes, and when each man had reloaded his ass they returned to the city. 14. When Judah and his brothers arrived at Joseph's house he was still there, so they fell on the ground in front of him. 15. 'What is this deed you have done?' Joseph asked them. 'Did you not know that a man such as I am is a reader of omens?' 16. 'What can we answer my lord?' Judah replied 'What can we say? How can we clear ourselves? God himself has uncovered your servants' guilt. Here we are then, my lord's slaves, we no less than the one in whose possession the cup was found.' 17. 'I could not think of doing such a thing' he replied. 'The man in whose possession the cup was found shall be my slave, but you can go back safe and sound to your father.' 18. Then Judah went up to him and said, 'May it please my lord, let your servant have a word privately with my lord. Do not be angry with your servant, for you are like Pharaoh himself. 19. My lord questioned his servants, "Have you father or brother?" 20. And we said to my lord, "We have an old father, and a younger brother born of his old age. His brother is dead, so he is the only one left of his mother, and his father loves him." 21. Then you said to your servants, "Bring him down to me that my eyes may look on him". 22. We replied to my lord, "The boy cannot leave his father. If he leaves him, his father will die." 23. But you said to your servants, "If your youngest brother does not come down with you, will you not be admitted to my presence again". 24. When we went back to your servant my father, we repeated to him what my lord had said. 25. So when our father said, "Go back and buy us a little food", 26. we said, "We cannot go down. If our youngest brother is with us, we will go down, for we cannot be admitted to the man's presence unless our youngest brother is with us." 27. So your servant our father said to us, "You know that my wife bore me two children. 28. When one left me, I said that he must have been torn to pieces And I have not seen him to this day. 29. If you take this one from me too and any harm comes to him, you will send me down to Sheol with my white head bowed in misery." 30. If I to your servant my father now, and we have not the boy with us, he will die as soon as he sees the boy is not with us, for his heart is bound up with him. 31. Then your servants will have sent your servant our father down to Sheol with his white head bowed in grief. 32. Now your servant went surety to my father for the boy. I said: If I do not bring him back to you, let me bear the blame before may father all my life. 33. Let your servant stay, then, as my lord's slave in place of the boy, I implore you, and let the boy go back with his brothers. 34. How indeed could I go back to my father and not have the boy with me? I could not bear to see the misery that would over-whelm my father.'

JOSEPH REVEALS HIMSELF

⟨∿⟩ CHAPTER 45. 1. Then Joseph could not control his feelings in front of all his retainers, and he exclaimed, 'Let everyone leave me'. No one therefore was present with him while Joseph made himself known to his brothers, 2. but he wept so loudly that all the Egyptians heard, and the news reached Pharaoh's palace. 3. Joseph said to his brothers, 'I am Joseph. Is my father really still alive?' His brothers could not answer him, they were so dismayed at the sight of him. 4. Then Joseph said to his brothers, 'Come closer to me'. When they had come closer to him he said, 'I am your brother Joseph whom you sold into Egypt. 5. But now, do not grieve, do not reproach yourselves for having sold me here, since God sent me before you to preserve your lives. 6. For this is the second year there has been famine in the country, and there are still five years to come of no ploughing or reaping. 7. God sent me before you to make sure that your race would have survivors in the land and to save your lives, many lives at that. 8. So it was not you who sent me here but God, and he has made me father to Pharaoh, lord of all his household and administrator of the whole land of Egypt. 9. 'Return quickly to your father and tell him, "Your son Joseph says this: God has made me lord of all Egypt. Come down to me at once. 10. You shall live in the country of Goshen where you will be near me, you, your children and your grandchildren, your flocks, your cattle and all your possessions. 11. I will provide for you there, for there are still five years of famine, and I do not want you to be in need, you and your household and all you have." 12. You can see with your own eyes, and my brother Benjamin can see too that it is my own mouth speaking to you. 13. Give my father a full report of all the honour I enjoy in Egypt, and of all you have seen. Then hurry and bring my father down here.' 14. Then throwing his arms round the neck of his brother Benjamin he wept; and Benjamin wept on his shoulder. 15. He kissed all his brothers, weeping over them. After which his brothers talked with him. 16. News reached Pharaoh's palace that Joseph's brothers had come, and Pharaoh was pleased to hear it, as were his servants. 17. Pharaoh told Joseph, 'Say to your brothers, "Do this: load your beasts and go off to the land of Canaan. 18. Fetch your father and families, and come back to me. I will give you the best the land of Egypt offers, and you shall feed on the fat of the land." 19. And you, for your part, give them this command: "Do this: take waggons from the land of Egypt, for your little ones and your wives. Get your father and come. 20. Never mind about your property, for the best that the land of Egypt offers is yours." ' 21. Israel's sons did as they were told. Joseph gave them waggons as Pharaoh had ordered, and he gave them provisions for the journey. 22. To each and every one he gave a festal garment, and to Benjamin three hundred shekels of silver and five festal garments. 23. And he sent his father ten donkeys laden with the best that Egypt offered, and ten she-donkeys laden with grain, bread and food for his father's journey. 24. Then he sent his brothers on their way. His final words to them were, 'Do not be upset on the journey'. 25. And so they left Egypt.

ISRAEL GOES DOWN TO EGYPT

When they reached the land of Canaan and their father Jacob, 26. they gave him this report, 'Joseph is still alive. Indeed it is he who is administrator of the whole land of Egypt.' But he was as one stunned, for he did not believe them. 27. However, when they told him all Joseph had said to them, and when he saw the waggons that Joseph had sent to fetch him, the spirit of their father Jacob revived, 28. and Israel said, 'That is enough! My son Joseph is still alive. I must go and see him before I die.'

CHAPTER 46. 1. Israel left with his possessions, and reached Beersheba. There he offered sacrifices to the God of his father Isaac. 2. God spoke to Israel in a vision at night, 'Jacob, Jacob', he said. 'I am here', he replied. 3. 'I am God, the God of your father', he continued. 'Do not be afraid of going down to Egypt, for I will make you a great nation there. 4. I myself will go down to Egypt with you. I myself will bring you back again, and Joseph's hand shall close your eyes.' 5. Then Jacob left Beersheba. Israel's sons conveyed their father Jacob, their little children and their wives in the waggons Pharaoh had sent to fetch him. 6. Taking their livestock and all that they had acquired in the land of Canaan, they went to Egypt, Jacob and all his family with him: 7. his sons and his grandsons, his daughters and his grand-daughters, in a word, all his children he took with him to Egypt. 8. These are the names of Israel's sons who came to Egypt, Reuben, Jacob's first-born, 9. and the sons of Reuben: Hanoch, Pallu, Hezron, Carmi. 10. The sons of Simeon: Jemuel, Jamin, Ohad, Jachin, Zohar, and Shaul the son of the Canaanite woman. 11. The sons of Levi: Gershon, Kohath, Merari. 12. The sons of Judah: Er, Onan, Shelah, Perez, and Zerah (though Er and Onan died in the land of Canaan), and Hezron and Hamul, sons of Perez. 13. The sons of Issachar: Tola, Puvah, Jashub and Shimron. 14. The sons of Zebulun: Sered, Elon, Jahleel. 15. These are the sons that Leah had born to Jacob in Paddan-aram, besides his daughter Dinah; in all, his sons and daughters numbered thirty-three. 16. The sons of Gad: Ziphion, Haggi, Shuni, Ezbon, Eri, Arodi, and Areli. 17. The sons of Asher: Imnah, Ishvah, Ishvi, Beriah, with their sister Serah; the sons of Beriah: Heber and Malchiel. 18. These are the sons of Zilpah whom Laban gave to his daughter Leah; she bore these to Jacob—sixteen persons. 19. The sons of Rachel, wife of Jacob: Joseph and Benjamin. 20. Born to Joseph in Egypt were: Manasseh and Ephraim, children of Asenath, the daughter of Poti-phera priest of On. 21. The sons of Benjamin: Bela, Becher, Ashbel, Gera, Naaman, Ehi, Rosh, Muppim, Huppim and Ard. 22. These are the sons that Rachel bore to Jacob—fourteen persons in all. 23. The sons of Dan: Hushim. 24. The sons of Naphtali: Jahzeel, Guni, Jezer and Shillem. 25. These are the sons of Bilhah whom Laban gave to his daughter Rachel; she bore these to Jacob—seven persons in all. 26. The people who went to Egypt with Jacob, of his own blood and not counting the wives of Jacob's sons, numbered sixty-six all told. 27. Joseph's sons born to him in Egypt were two in number. The members of the family of Jacob who went to Egypt totalled seventy.

JOSEPH IS RESTORED TO ISRAEL

28. Israel sent Judah ahead to Joseph, so that the latter might present himself to him in Goshen. When they arrived in the land of Goshen, 29. Joseph had his chariot made ready and went up to meet his father Israel in Goshen. As soon as he appeared he threw his arms round his neck and for a long time wept on his shoulder. 30. Israel said to Joseph, 'Now I can die, now that I have seen you again, and seen you still alive'. 31. Then Joseph said to his brothers and his father's family, 'I will go up and break the news to Pharaoh. I will tell him, "My brothers and my father's family who were in the land of Canaan have come to me. 32. The men are shepherds and look after livestock, and they have brought their flocks and cattle and all their possessions." 33. Thus, when Pharaoh summons you and asks, "What is your occupation?", 34. you are to say, "Ever since our boyhood your servants have looked after livestock, we and our fathers before us". And so you will be able to stay in the land of Goshen.' For the Egyptians have a horror of all shepherds.

JOSEPH AND ISRAEL BEFORE PHARAOH

CHAPTER 47. 1. So Joseph went and told Pharaoh, 'My father and brothers, along with their flocks and cattle and all their possessions, have come from the land of Canaan and are now in the land of Goshen'. 2. He had taken five of his brothers, and he now presented them to Pharaoh. 3. Pharaoh asked his brothers, 'What is your occupation?' and they gave Pharaoh the answer, 'Your servants are shepherds, like our fathers before us'. 4. They went on to tell Pharaoh, 'We have come to stay for the present in this land, for there is no pasture for your servant's flocks, the land of Canaan is hard-pressed by famine. Now give your servants leave to stay in the land of Goshen.' 5. Then Pharaoh said to Joseph, 6. 'They may stay in the land of Goshen, and if you know of any capable men among them, put them in charge of my own livestock'. 7. Joseph brought his father and presented him to Pharaoh. Jacob blessed Pharaoh. 8. Pharaoh asked Jacob, 'How many years of life can you reckon?' 9. 'My life of wandering has lasted one hundred and thirty years,' Jacob told

Pharaoh 'few years and unhappy, falling short of the years of my fathers in their life of wandering.' 10.· Jacob blessed Pharaoh and left Pharaoh's presence. 11. Joseph settled his father and brothers, giving them a holding in the land of Egypt, and in the best region of the land, namely the land of Rameses, according to Pharaoh's command. 12. Joseph provided his father, brothers and all his father's family with food according to the number of their dependants. 13. There was no bread in the whole land, for the famine had grown so severe that the land of Egypt and the land of Canaan were weakened with hunger. 14. Joseph accumulated all the money there was to be found in the land of Egypt and in the land of Canaan, in return for the grain which men were buying, and he brought the money to Pharaoh's palace. 15. When all the money in the land of Egypt and in the land of Canaan had run out, the Egyptians all came to Joseph: 'Give us bread' they said. 'Have we to perish before your eyes? For our money has come to an end.' 16. Joseph answered, 'Hand over your livestock; I am willing to give you bread in exchange for your livestock, if your money has come to an end'. 17. So they brought their livestock to Joseph, and Joseph gave them bread, in exchange for horses and livestock, whether sheep or cattle, and for donkeys. Thus he fed them that year with bread, in exchange for all their livestock. 18. When that year was over, they came to him the next year, and said to him, 'We cannot hide it from my lord: the truth is, our money has run out and the livestock is in my lord's possession. There is nothing left for my lord except our bodies and our land. 19. Have we to perish before your eyes, we and our land? Buy us and our land in exchange for bread: we with our land will be Pharaoh's serfs. But give us something to sow, that we may keep our lives and not die and the land may not become desolate.' 20. Thus Joseph acquired all the land in Egypt for Pharaoh, since one by one the Egyptians sold their estates, so hard-pressed were they by the famine, and the whole country passed into Pharaoh's possession. 21. As for the people, he reduced them to serfdom from one end of Egypt to the other. 22. The only land he did not acquire belonged to the priests, for the priests received an allowance

ISRAEL BLESSES JOSEPH'S SONS

CHAPTER 48. 1. Some time later it was reported to Joseph, 'Your father has been taken ill'. So he took with him his two sons Manasseh and Ephraim. 2. When Jacob was told, 'Look, your son Joseph has come to you', Israel, summoning his strength, sat up in bed. 3. 'El Shaddai appeared to me at Luz in the country of Canaan,' Jacob told Joseph 'and he blessed me, 4. saying to me, "I will make you fruitful and increase you in numbers. I will make you a group of peoples and give this country to your descendants after you, to own in perpetuity." 5. Now your two sons, born to you in the land of Egypt before I came to you in Egypt, shall be mine; Ephraim and Manasseh shall be as much mine as Reuben and Simeon. 6. But with regard to the children you have had since them, they shall be yours, and they shall be known by their brothers' names for the purpose of their inheritance. 7. 'When I was on my way from Paddan, to my sorrow death took your mother Rachel from me, in the land of Canaan, on the journey while we were still some distance from Ephrath. I buried her there on the road to Ephrath at Bethlehem.' 8. When Israel saw Joseph's two sons, he asked, 'Who are these?' 9. 'They are my sons, whom God has given me here' Joseph told his father. 'Then bring them to me,' he said 'that I may bless them.' 10. Israel's sight was failing because of his great age, and so he could not see. Joseph therefore made them come closer to him and he kissed and embraced them. 11. Then Israel said to Joseph, 'I did not think that I should see you again, but God has let me see your family as well'. 12. Joseph took them from his lap and bowed to the ground. 13. Joseph took hold of the two of them, Ephraim with his right hand so that he should be on Israel's left, and Manasseh with his left hand, so that he should be on Israel's right, and brought them close to him. 14. But Israel held out his right hand and laid it on the head of Ephraim, the younger, and his left on the head of Manasseh, crossing his hands—Manasseh was, in fact, the elder. 15. Then he blessed Joseph saying: 'May God in whose presence my fathers Abraham and Isaac walked, may God who has been my shepherd from my birth until this day, 16. may the angel who has been my saviour from all harm, bless these boys, may my name live on in them, and the names of my fathers Abraham and Isaac. May they grow and increase on the earth.' 17. Joseph saw that his father was laying his right hand on the head of Ephraim, and this upset him. He took his father's hand and tried to shift it from the head of Ephraim to the head of Manasseh. 18. Joseph protested to his father, 'Not like that, father! This one is the elder; put your right hand on his head.' 19. But his father refused. 'I know, my son, I know' he said. 'He too shall become a people; he too shall be great. Yet his younger brother shall be greater than he, and his descendants shall become a multitude of nations.' 20. So he blessed them that day saying: 'May you be a blessing in Israel; may they say, "God make you like Ephraim and Manasseh!"' In this way he put Ephraim before Manasseh. 21. Then Israel said to Joseph, 'Now I am about to die. But God will be with you and take you back to the country of your fathers. 22. As for me, I give you a Shechem more than your brothers, the one I took from the Amorites with my sword and my bow.'

THE TESTAMENT OF ISRAEL

CHAPTER 49. 1. Jacob called his sons and said, 'Gather together that I may declare to you what lies before you in time to come. 2. Gather round, sons of Jacob, and listen; listen to Israel your father. 3. Reuben, you are my first-born, my vigour, and the first-fruit of my manhood, foremost in pride, foremost in strength, 4. uncontrolled as a flood: you shall not be foremost, for you mounted your father's bed, and so defiled my couch, to my hurt. 5. Simeon and Levi are brothers, they carried out their malicious plans. 6. Let my soul not enter into their counsel nor my heart join in their company, for in their rage they have killed men, in their fury they hamstrung bulls. 7. Accursed be their rage for its ruthlessness, their wrath for its ferocity. I will divide them among Jacob, I will scatter them among Israel. 8. Judah, your brothers shall praise you: you grip your enemies by the neck, your father's sons shall do you homage, 9. Judah is a lion cub, you climb back, my son, from your kill; like a lion he crouches and lies down, or a lioness: who dare rouse him? 10. The sceptre shall not pass from Judah, nor the mace from between his feet, until he come to whom it belongs, to whom the peoples shall render obedience. 11. He ties up his young ass to the vine, to its stock the foal of his she-ass. He washes his coat in wine, his cloak in the blood of the grape; 12. his eyes are cloudy with wine, his teeth are white with milk. 13. Zebulun lives by the shore of the sea, he is a sailor on board the ships, he has Sidon close by him. 14. Issachar is a strong ass, lying down in the midst of the sheepfolds. 15. He saw how good it was to take his ease, how pleasant was the country, so he bowed his shoulders for the load, he became a slave to forced labour. 16. Dan is judge of his people like each one of the tribes of Israel. 17. May Dan be a serpent on the road, a viper on the path, who bites the horse on the hock and its rider falls backward. 18. I trust in your salvation, Yahweh. 19. Gad, robbers rob him, and he, he robs and pursues them. 20. Asher, his bread is rich, he provides food fit for a king. 21. Naphtali is a swift hind, dropping beautiful fawns. 22. Joseph is a fruitful creeper near the spring, whose tendrils climb over the wall. 23. Bowmen provoked him, they drew and assailed him. 24. But their bow was broken by a mighty one, the sinews of their arms were parted by the hands of the Mighty One of Jacob, by the name of the Stone of Israel, 25. by the God of your father who assists you, by El Shaddai who blesses you: with blessings of heaven above, blessings of the deep lying below, blessings of breasts and womb, 26. blessings of grain and flowers, blessings of ancient mountains; bounty of the everlasting hills; may they descend on Joseph's head, on the brow of the dedicated one among his brothers. 27. Benjamin is a ravening wolf, in the morning he devours his prey, in the evening he is still dividing the spoil.' 28. All these make up the tribes of Israel, twelve in number, and this is what their father said to them. He blessed them, giving to each one an appropriate blessing. 29. Then he gave them these instructions, 'I am about to be gathered to my people. Bury me near my fathers, in the cave that is in the field of Ephron the Hittite, 30. in the cave in the field at Machpelah, opposite Mamre, in the land of Canaan, which Abraham bought from Ephron the Hittite as a burial-plot.

THE DEATH OF ISRAEL

31. There Abraham was buried and his wife Sarah. There Isaac was buried and his wife Rebekah. There I buried Leah. 32. I mean the field and the cave in it that were bought from the sons of Heth.' 33. When Jacob had finished giving his instructions to his sons, he drew his feet up into the bed, and breathing his last was gathered to his people.

CHAPTER 50. 1. At this Joseph threw himself on his father, covering his face with tears and kissing him. 2. Then Joseph ordered the doctors in his service to embalm his father. The doctors embalmed Israel, 3. and it took them forty days, for embalming takes forty days to complete. The Egyptians mourned him for seventy days. 4. When the period of mourning for him was over, Joseph said to Pharaoh's household, 'If I may presume to enjoy your favour, please see that this message reaches Pharaoh's ears, 5. "My father made me swear an oath: I am about to die, he said, I have a tomb which I dug for myself in the land of Canaan, and there you must bury me. So now I seek leave to go up and bury my father, and then I shall come back." '

ISRAEL'S BURIAL

6. Pharaoh replied, 'Go up and bury your father, in accordance with the oath he made you swear'. 7. Joseph went up to bury his father, all Pharaoh's servants and the palace dignitaries going up with him, joined by all the dignitaries of the land of Egypt, 8. as well as all Joseph's family and his brothers, along with his father's family. They left no one in the land of Goshen but their dependants, with their flocks and their cattle. 9. Chariots also and horsemen went up with them; it was a very large retinue. 10. On arriving at Goren-ha-atad, which is across the Jordan, they performed there a long and solemn lamentation, and Joseph observed three days' mourning for his father. 11. When the Canaanites, the inhabitants of the land, witnessed the mourning at Goren-ha-atad they exclaimed, 'This is a solemn act of mourning for the Egyptians'. For this reason they call this place Abel-mizraim—it is across the Jordan. 12. His sons did what he had ordered them to do for him. 13. His sons carried him to the land of Canaan and buried him in the cave in the field at Machpelah opposite Mamre,

from Pharaoh and lived on the allowance that Pharaoh gave them. Therefore they did not have to sell their land. 23. Then Joseph said to the people, This is how we stand: I have bought you out, with your land, on Pharaoh's behalf. Here is seed for you so that you can sow the land. 24. But when harvest comes you must give a fifth to Pharaoh. The other four-fifths you can have for sowing your fields, to provide food for yourselves and your households, and food for your dependants.' 25. 'You have saved our lives' they replied. 'If we may enjoy my lord's favour, we will be Pharaoh's serfs.' 26. So Joseph made a statute, still in force today, concerning the soil of Egypt: a fifth goes to Pharaoh. The land of the priests alone did not go to Pharaoh. 27. The Israelites stayed in the land of Egypt, in the country of Goshen. They acquired property there; they were fruitful and increased in numbers greatly. 28. Jacob lived seventeen years in the land of Egypt, and the length of his life was a hundred and forty-seven years. 29. When Israel's time to die drew near he called his son Joseph and said to him, 'If I enjoy your favour, place your hand under my thigh and promise to be kind and good to me, do not bury me in Egypt. 30. When I sleep with my fathers, carry me out of Egypt and bury me in their tomb.' 'I will do as you say' he replied. 31. 'Swear to me' he insisted. So he swore to him, and Israel sank back on the pillow.

which Abraham had bought from Ephron the Hittite
as a burial-plot.

JOSEPH'S BROTHERS ASK
FOREGIVENESS

14. Then Joseph returned to Egypt, he and his brothers, along with all those who had come up with him for his father's burial. 15. Seeing that their father was dead, Joseph's brothers said, 'What if Joseph intends to treat us as enemies and repay us in full for all the wrong we did him?' 16. So they sent this message to Joseph: 'Before your father died he gave us this order: 17. "You must say to Joseph: Oh forgive your brothers their crime and their sin and all the wrong they did you". Now therefore, we beg you, forgive the crime of the servants of your father's God.' Joseph wept at the message they sent to him. 18. His brothers came themselves and fell down before him. 'We present ourselves before you' they said 'as your slaves.' 19. But Joseph answered them, 'Do not be afraid; is it for me to put myself in God's place? 20. The evil you planned to do me has by God's design been turned to good, that he might bring about, as indeed he has, the deliverance of a numerous people. 21. So you need not be afraid; I

myself will provide for you and your dependants.' In this way he reassured them with words that touched their hearts.

JOSEPH'S BROTHERS SWEAR AN OATH

22. So Joseph stayed in Egypt with his father's family; and Joseph lived a hundred and ten years. 23. Joseph saw the third generation of Ephraim's children, as also the children of Machir, Manasseh's son, who were born on Joseph's lap. 24. At length Joseph said to his brothers, 'I am about to die; but God will be sure to remember you kindly and take you back from this country to the land that he promised on oath to Abraham, Isaac and Jacob'. 25. And Joseph made Israel's sons swear an oath, 'When God remembers you with kindness be sure to take my bones from here'.

JOSEPH DIES IN EGYPT

26. Joseph died at the age of a hundred and ten; they
embalmed him and laid him in his coffin in Egypt.

THE ARTIST:
HERMANN FECHENBACH

The tragic vicissitudes of the present times are re-
flected with singular vividness in the life and experi-
ences of the artist. In this sense, his case is a typical
one; but the individual note is discernible in the way
in which the gifted artist, so far from becoming
a victim of circumstances, has drawn additional
strength and inspiration from them.

Born 1897 in Bad Mergentheim Wurttemberg,
Hermann Fechenbach took part, while still a very
young man, in the first world war. He was severely
wounded in August 1917, as a result suffering the
loss of one leg; but no handicaps could ever alter his
determination to follow his vocation as an artist. He
studied art at the Academies in Stuttgart, Munich,
Florence and Vienna from 1919-1926.

Hard work brought him well-earned successes in Germany, Austria, Italy, Palestine and England.

The chain of circumstances forced him to emigrate
from Germany, settling in England in 1939. In March
1944, he came to live in London, where he has been
continuously at work ever since.

The district from which he springs and where his
talent was formed has long figured in history as a
centre whose art and craftsmanship have been able
to develop with exceptional felicity. Though a pain-
ter in the first instance — in ambition as well as
achievement — Fechenbach has also done a great deal
of work in black and white, showing his mastery of
many mediums; and his work as a woodcarver has
also produced notable results.

This many-sided artist, subtle and convincing as
interpreter of human psychology, also shows a re-
markable gift for catching the genius loci — his land-
scapes, inspired by many countries, bear eloquent
witness in this respect. And whatever he touches he
makes us feel that he stands on firm ground of true
European civilisation, as it echoed through the cen-
turies — a fact which gives his work a moral back-
ground of profound significance, entirely apart from
what he has achieved as an artist in the immediate
sense of the word.

Tancred Borenius